A NOVEL BY

NIKOS KAZANTZAKIS

Translated from the French by
RICHARD HOWARD

Passages from *The Saviors of God* translated by
KIMON FRIAR

A TOUCHSTONE BOOK PUBLISHED BY
SIMON AND SCHUSTER

Rock Garden

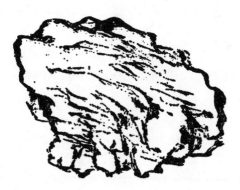

PUBLISHERS' NOTE

Certain portions of The Rock Garden *are, in fact, passages from Nikos Kazantzakis'* The Saviors of God: Spiritual Exercises, *and some few selections from his travel book* Japan-China. *Partly because he wanted to make* The Saviors of God *available to a wider audience, and partly because its meaning was sharpened for him by his contact with the East, Kazantzakis included in the novel many significant fragments of the earlier book. In a sense, the novel itself is almost an illustration of the philosophy contained in* The Saviors of God, *and the story of Joshiro, Li-Te, and Siu-lan is a reflection of Kazantzakis' ideas.*

Kazantzakis wrote The Rock Garden—*in French—in the first months of 1936 on his return from the East, but he had written* The Saviors of God—*in Greek—during the last month of 1922 and the first five months of 1923, and published it in the Greek periodical* Renaissance *in 1927. In 1936 he himself translated into French those portions of* The Saviors of God *which he wished to include in his novel, but the publisher, Grethlein of Leipzig, found himself unable to publish it because of the Nazi regime. Nevertheless, it was first published in Dutch (Nicolai Kazantzaki,* De Tuin der Rotsen, *translated by R. Blijstra, Wereldbiblio-*

3

theek, Amsterdam, 1939); and in Spanish, in Chile (Nicolás Kazan, El Jardín de las Rocas, translated by Hernán del Solar, Ercilla Santiago, 1941).

It was not until 1958 that a French typescript of the original manuscript (since lost) was found among Kazantzakis' papers after his death. This was published in Paris in 1959 by Librairie Plon (Nikos Kazantzaki, Le Jardin des Rochers, *with a Preface by Aziz Izzet). A corrected version of the French typescript was then translated into Greek by Pandelis Prevelakis (author of* Nikos Kazantzakis and His Odyssey: A Study of the Poet and the Poem, *Simon and Schuster, 1961) with an Introduction, and published in Athens in 1960. Kazantzakis, in the meantime, had made a definitive revision of* The Saviors of God *in Greek, and this had been published in book form under Mr. Prevelakis' supervision in 1945 in Athens. In his translation of* The Rock Garden *from French into Greek, Mr. Prevelakis of course inserted Kazantzakis' final revision of* The Saviors of God *in Greek, but followed the order and adaptation as indicated by Kazantzakis in the French typescript. It is this order and this adaptation which is followed here.*

The 1945 final version of The Saviors of God: Spiritual Exercises *was translated from the Greek by Kimon Friar, supplied with Notes and Introduction, and published by Simon and Schuster in 1960. It is indispensable for the full understanding of Kazantzakis' work and thought, for it contains the core of the philosophy which all his books mirror, no matter what their form. In particular, it exists in another transformation in Books XIV and XVI of* The Odyssey: A Modern Sequel (*translated by Kimon Friar, with Introduction, Notes, and Synopsis, Simon and Schuster, 1958). For the convenience of the reader and student of Kazantzakis' works, we have thought it best to use Mr. Friar's translation of those passages of* The Rock Garden *which Kazantzakis took from* The Saviors of God. *They appear throughout this novel in italics and follow the order and adaptation used by Mr. Prevelakis.*

4

The Rock Garden

1

"H<small>ELP!</small>"

Suddenly a harsh, muffled cry from the depths pierced my heart.

Yet I was so happy! A deep, mute, motionless happiness like that of a tiny insect warming itself in the sun.

Had not this whole pilgrimage to Japan been one long enchantment? What else could my insatiable and ungrateful heart desire?

Like an old *biku* who leaves his sons, his grandsons, and vanishes into the forest, like a grub that takes refuge in solitude at the mercy of the mysterious itch of nascent wings I vanished into Japan.

A critical moment of my life, a vague and profound anxiety—the malaise of impending change.

I was smothering—women, ideas, political action. . . . Travel? I chose travel as my road to salvation.

From birth I have thirsted for the abyss, for annihilation, for a drop of deadly Oriental poison, and I had finally decided to cure myself of that craving.

How? By burying myself deep in that deleterious East, by filling my eyes with all the Buddha-like smiles that mesmerize and murder hope on earth.

To unite the various secret voices that rise from deep within me, proclaiming the irremediable catastrophe of all human effort, to give form to this chaos, to find the laws of this anarchy, to impose order on the confusion of my desires—such was the hidden goal of this long pilgrimage.

Thus might I master these feline voices and remain alone with my naïve peasant heart that tills and sows the void, ignorant of its fate, and ignorantly, by degrees, creates, with all creative hearts, the impossible.

Someone in me is suffering and struggling toward freedom. I would rid my soul of all the weeds invading it. Sitting in the profound calm of the Japanese gardens around the swarming staircases of temples, I would trace the route of my inner pilgrim, of the Great Stranger, and mark the stages along the way.

In the tremor of immobility which musters its strength before it springs, I prepare myself for the journey. Preparation, departure, journey, journey's goal, arrival—I am determined to find the secret meaning of every stage and capture it in words.

Japan, its terrible passions subject to a disciplined and smiling form, will be my guide. Terra incognita, everything there will seem virgin to me: the shock will be strong.

I knew only two Japanese words when I embarked for this great chrysanthemum: *sakura*, cherry blossom, and *kokoro*, heart. These two words, I told myself, will be the two keys that will open every door. How could I have known I would need a third word, whose Japanese equivalent I did not yet know? In my language, the word is:

Terror.

The blue sea, the gulls, the spring clouds, the dolphins—intense, violent, the vision invades all my sense. Lurid colors, smooth and naked bodies, obscene and innocent whispers, succulent and rotting fruits, foul odors joyously mingling with the intoxicating perfume of jasmine. . . .

"Joshiro-san," I said to my companion aboard the ship taking us to Japan. "Joshiro-san, your soul, surely, is very simple, like every woman's soul; your body, like every woman's body, whether white, yellow, or black, is eager for caresses. I know all the naked mysteries, but you are of another race than I, and that eagerly arouses my curiosity. The voyage is too long; suppose we make love a little, Joshiro-san?"

A broad Buddha-like smile appeared on her heavy lips and spread across the width of her coarse but polished yellow face.

And as she said nothing, her long, oblique eyes staring over the yellow sea, I continued, laughing:

"What luck! Through you, Joshiro-san, I might understand the yellow race better than by reading all the volumes ever written about this fascinating and dangerous people. Love is the greatest pedagogue; its method is the surest, for it is based on our most intimate senses—touch and smell."

Joshiro laughed and gave me a long look, her teeth flashing in the Eastern sun; the green sea of Egypt already stretched before us like a tender field in spring.

The passengers were playing miniature golf, shuffleboard, chess; they stuffed themselves with food, told each other dirty stories; the women listened, ears cocked. Every day they undressed a little more, reveling in the heat, their accomplice.

Joshiro, lying on her deck chair, inhaled the salt air greedily; like a cat she luxuriated in the morning sun.

Suddenly I was ashamed of my lascivious glances, my shameless words; I stood up.

Joshiro was unendurable. She had lost the delicate but disturbing charm of the Japanese women, her naïve smile, her insinuating grace—the omnipotence of weakness. She had become, with her sports clothes and her emancipated woman's freedom, a hybrid, equivocal being, half ridiculous, half tragic, like all the incoherent organisms of transition.

9

She was unendurable, yet something about her attracted me—perhaps her yellow skin which was so smooth and her long, narrow eyes, and, above all, the odor that emanated from her body these last hot days—an animal odor of musk.

"The loveliest moment and you're leaving? Where are you going?"

"To get a breath of air."

Before me stretched the Egyptian sea, and on the horizon, a rippling, misty line—land.

A song of suffering from the age of Pharaohs suddenly pierced my heart. Tossed by the fever of our time, a great tide rises within us, rises and reddens. . . . All we can understand now is anguish.

I ignore the kings and gods, the victories, the profound mysteries of this land rising before me, and I keep only the cry of a poor cross-legged, motionless scribe who saw the suffering and raised his voice:

"I have seen! I have seen! I have seen! I have seen the blacksmiths; their fingers are hard as the skin of the crocodile. . . . I have seen the laborers who water the ground with their sweat. Sickness lies in wait for the masons—all day under the burning sun they work, clinging to the roofs; at night they return to their homes and beat their wives and children. I have seen the weaver with his knees nailed to his belly; I have seen the messenger who trembles as he sets out for the desert. . . .

"I have seen! I have seen! I have seen!"

I listened to the scribe, the implacable witness, and my heart was shaken. To flirt with Joshiro, to waste time's precious essence in vain words—how shameful! Before me, the scribe rose out of this earth, his eyes wide, his hand raised, ready to trace the irrefutable words—"I see! I see! I see!" Suddenly, all the suffering of our time bursts like an abscess before my eyes.

Joshiro had followed me—the sweat beaded like dew on her upper lip; her marcelled hair was plastered on the back of her neck now. The odor of her strong, supple body filled me with a degrading intoxication.

"What are you thinking about?" she murmured, recovering her feminine intonations. She had forgotten her boyish ways and her enlightened independence; she had become a true woman again, faithful to her high mission of drowning man's spirit.

"I am thinking about suffering," I answered, trying to shake off the gentle torpor that was overcoming me. But at the odor of this young, unknown body, I floundered.

Someone within me grew enraged. Joshiro sighed. I turned around.

"Don't sigh," I said harshly, "you can't understand. Have you ever suffered?"

Joshiro's eyes sparkled. "Yes," she answered in a low voice. "Li-Te?"

At this name a shudder ran over Joshiro's bare shoulders. She did not answer. Her face had grown very pale and rigid as a mask of fear. Her lips, pressed together, vanished.

"Forgive me, Joshiro-san," I murmured.

She did not hear me. Motionless, she stared at the sea.

I had touched a wound that had not healed. The taciturn Chinese boy Li-Te, my friend at Oxford, had loved her once, passionately, and then he had abruptly abandoned her and returned to China.

Joshiro had come to me for help that very evening.

"Don't let me kill myself!" she had cried, collapsing on my doorstep. "Don't let me kill myself! I want to live for revenge!"

She had fallen seriously ill. She spat blood and the doctors shrugged their shoulders, unable to do anything for her, but Joshiro would not die. Lying on the huge white pillows, she stared at us, smiling.

"Don't worry!" she had said. "Don't worry, I won't die."

She recovered, got out of bed, and began working in desperation at the Japanese Embassy in London. She often went to Japan and clandestinely visited Manchuria, disguised as a Chinese.

What was she doing? She never told anyone. The name Li-Te never passed her wide, sensual lips.

11

Had she forgotten? She slept with men and abandoned them the next day with a kind of joyous cruelty. Her remarks were often cynical. Surely, I decided each time I saw her, she must have forgotten my friend and her revenge.

And today she stiffened at the mention of Li-Te's name, implacable as ever.

"Joshiro-san," I repeated in a low voice. "Forgive me."

"Shut up!" she exclaimed harshly. "Shut up!"

2

*N*OON WAS ALREADY showering us with its vertical arrows. The ship lowered its gangway to the dockside. Joshiro did not answer when I called her.

I disembarked alone and wandered down the quay, nostrils wide. Avidly I inhaled the air, saturated with the odors of the Oriental port. I ate mangoes and bananas, chewed betel nuts, whistled, laughed to myself; I was happy.

I thanked the blind force that had given me life and led me to wander here, to smell the acrid odor of young flesh, to caress slowly, lovingly, the forbidden fruit.

The harbors of the Orient smell of musk, like animals in heat. Savage, sensual, they open their arms to the depths of a golden sea, and the poisons they sell are sweet.

> *Are the harbor girls anchors or ropes?*
> *Just this morning*
> *They kept two boats in port!*

I whistled this *haiku* on the quay of Port Saïd, my hands full of bananas.

A heavy-set, austere American was walking solemnly a few steps ahead of me. He wore a black cap with SALVATION ARMY stitched on it in mauve.

Fanatical, hideously virtuous, his eyes cold and hard—what was this Christian after, here in this motley harbor overflowing with sun, fruit and little half-naked sirens? Never have I seen a stare so filled with hate, so inaccessible to the Orient and to love. He glared at the poor painted girls—his sisters—and his eyes brimmed with venom.

Without mauve letters on my cap, without a cap, my pipe clenched tight between my teeth, I followed this man of the North, washed up on these sunny shores.

Suddenly a little chocolate-colored boy dashed out of the shadows. His eyes were laughing, his henna-reddened nails sparkled in the sunlight. He clung to the blue-eyed Christian's jacket.

"*Moussiou . . . Moussiou . . .*"

I didn't hear what he said, but I was sure he was offering the same merchandise he had offered me five minutes before.

"*Moussiou . . . Moussiou . . .* a nice fat little girl . . . nice and fat . . . my sister . . . you come!"

And when I had turned around laughing and said: "I don't want women!" the urchin unhesitatingly modified his merchandise.

"*Moussiou . . . Moussiou . . .* little boy . . . very pretty . . . very pretty . . . my brother! You come!"

"I don't want boys!"

He had looked at me in alarm and vanished into the darkness. Now here he was again, clinging to the sacred jacket.

"*Moussiou . . . Moussiou . . .*"

The Man of Virtue stopped, astonished, outraged.

"*Moussiou . . . Moussiou . . .*"

Suddenly the poor child, who had the divine innocence of some animal, was terrified. He had met the missionary's eyes and understood. He had instinctively grasped the hatred, the rage, the ice of virtue.

14

As if he had been playing in a grassy meadow and suddenly discovered a viper, head raised and staring at him, the child stood there, in the middle of the quay, gaping, terrified, and turned to me as if he were imploring my help.

I smiled at him; immediately he plucked up his courage and took a dozen obscene photographs out of his belt.

"*Moussiou . . . Moussiou . . .* photos! *Tsst! Tsst!* Look!"

To console the little human animal and revive his trust in humanity, I gave him the ten piasters he was asking and he skipped off into the shadows.

I sat down on the shore of this shameless sea and began to leaf through these obscene images. I heard the sea sighing where it lay naked on the strand, and I realized that here in the harbors of the Orient virtue might become voluptuous and hospitable; that sin has excuses and even an innocence unthinkable in the barbarous countries of the snow.

Dates, bananas, citrons, mangoes enjoyed a secret correspondence with the morality, the art and the ideas born in their shade. The fruits of these Oriental ports and their gods resemble each other like brothers.

It was time to leave, to sail into the Red Sea and its stifling heat. The only way to cool off was to think of the stokers in the ship's bowels.

I often caught Joshiro staring into the East, her eyes fixed. I sensed her strange impatience. I no longer dared talk about love or joke with her. Suddenly Joshiro had attained a greater importance. She spoke with the sailors and the officers. She quickly became the center of a tiny intense movement.

"Joshiro," I asked her, "don't you suffer from the heat?"

"No," she answered, smiling, "I'm thinking about Japan."

She was thinking about Japan; the minor details of life—heat, love—could no longer touch her. In a small place, life in common can become a real torment or a slow degradation if it is not inflamed by some great passion.

"Are you going to China too, Joshiro-san?"

A heavy-set Chinese was strolling ahead of us, laboriously

dragging his right leg. He had a scanty black beard and a deep scar cleft his forehead in two.

He heard my question and suddenly stopped. He sighed and sank down on a bench. With an indifferent expression he fixed his somnolent eyes on us.

"I don't know," Joshiro answered in a low voice, and added, "Please, don't speak so loud."

"Maybe I'll see you again—in China? Will you be staying there long?"

Joshiro's voice became a menacing whisper. I didn't understand why until much later, on a tragic day in China.

"Long?" she murmured. "Perhaps forever. . . ."

The limping Chinese closed his eyes; he must have fallen asleep. He began snoring gently.

We had stretched out on our deck chairs and were watching the pale pink mountains of Arabia slide past, very beautiful, very inhuman.

The sun was revolving heavily over our heads, like a millstone. White men and white women were beginning to decompose. A smell of corpses seeped from the cabins. The half-naked women were dying of boredom and languor; their morality was dissolving in the heat, melting like butter. Occasionally the English uttered some wild beast's cry and collapsed into inertia.

I watched my traveling companions, and sometimes my gaze was harsh, sometimes filled with pity. Once they had exchanged their stories, gambled, smoked, made love, they were emptied. Now they stirred—empty trousers, empty blouses: a loathsome human laundry on the ship's rigging, swollen in the wind.

Only a few Indian Moslems on deck still preserved their human dignity. Every morning at sunrise, every evening at sunset, they knelt on their mats and prayed. Their religion gave them a solar rhythm, made their soul a sunflower that follows the journey of our Father in heaven. If all the passengers were rotting, only these Moslems were resisting corruption.

At last one morning, at dawn—Colombo. A gentle hour, an amorous movement of the prow that in the morning's orange and purple vapors penetrates noiselessly into the sleeping city. . . . The sun explodes, the minarets rise up, flowering bougainvillaeas scale the walls; the alluring, perfumed sirens chewing betel nuts laugh and whisper in front of the indigo sea. A warm humanity that is not afraid of colors flocks out of the alleyways onto the quays: broad banana leaves, a handful of rice with red pepper scooped out by frail fingers with henna-red nails, and we eat in the shade.

A tiny bronze Buddha sitting on a stone at the crossroads. A prostrate old man tells it about his business; a young girl smiles and sets at its tiny feet a few red flowers, hibiscus with inflamed tongues. Around the Buddha's head, a dozen tiny bamboo windmills, the prayer wheels. For an instant the breeze blows and the mills laboriously begin grinding out men's desires.

The girl who had offered Buddha the red flowers looks at me with a smile and makes a sign. I follow the tinkle of the bronze rings she wears on one ankle. She leaves, joyously swaying her hips; she is happy, her prayer was answered promptly.

A door opens—a tiny courtyard, a dark bamboo room. The cool shade, the smell of maize and pepper. The anklets begin rattling noisily and the white teeth flash in a perfumed darkness.

Life is a very simple miracle, happiness is within the reach of all, made to man's measure; it lasts a moment and it is good.

We leave; we breathe that cool and chaste element, the sea. The soul finally masters itself; it is ashamed of all it has seen, heard, tasted and touched upon the earth. Alas, this soul is only a Christian maiden, still frightened, still terrified of the scarecrow hanging on the tree of life.

New harbors appear on the horizon, the human skin changes color; it has been dark and brown; it has taken on the color of chocolate and now it turns yellow. These human beings have descended from another monkey—one tiny and agile.

Night falls as suddenly as a sword. The air grows cooler. The many-colored lanterns are lit on all the lace balconies. The shops are closed, the stench abates a little, the evening flowers open. The yellow hands are full of roasted melon seeds and the crowds stroll through the gardens nibbling gently, gently as mice.

Joshiro, leaning over the prow, watched the flying fish of China pierce the waves like arrows from crest to crest.

At that moment she looked dangerous and beautiful; her hair, whipped about by the wind, gave her a fierce and sensual expression.

"Joshiro-san," I said, laughing, "in a few days the trip will be over and I'll have forgotten to make you my little declaration."

"Me too," she answered, bursting into laughter. "I forgot about my woman's mission: to cajole, to bemire the body, to suck men's souls . . . I had other fish to fry."

"China?" I asked, after a moment's hesitation.

"Yes. China," Joshiro answered in a low voice.

She continued: "Love is a very agreeable exercise, a rather ridiculous but rather sweet movement. I have greatly enjoyed it, I probably enjoy it still. But it can no longer give me happiness—by which I mean the sense that we're doing our duty. Today love can be nothing but the momentary pastime of heroes."

"And of heroines," I added, smiling.

"I'm no heroine," Joshiro murmured, suddenly sad and serious. "I haven't been able to give my life for my cause yet."

She stretched out her hand and pointed to distant China on the left. "But I still hope," she murmured.

"You hope for death?"

"Yes, fruitful death, more living than life. Death, the supreme love."

She fell silent; her eyes were fixed on the distance.

"We need strong souls," she continued abruptly. "We Japanese. Japan has the great responsibility of leading all Asia and of fighting . . ."

"For freedom?"

Joshiro reflected a moment; she smiled.

"Oh, you white men!" she said sarcastically. "You white men and your white ideas—freedom, equality, brotherhood . . . Christian chimeras . . . vegetarian virtues. China is ours!" she exclaimed, as if she had guessed my thoughts. "China is ours, and anyone else who touches her should beware!"

Her eyes filled with a strange mist; for a second I thought Joshiro was going to burst into tears.

In her passionate soul, China must have been inseparably linked to her love for Li-Te. Joshiro must have taken a profoundly personal joy impelling her own race to conquer China. For her, conquest and vengeance had the same face.

The limping Chinese passed us again, painfully dragging his right leg; he stopped for a moment, out of breath. He was listening.

Joshiro stared at him and frowned; again she began watching the fish flying toward China, and she forgot my presence.

"What is it you like about talking to Japanese people?" whispered one of my traveling companions who was proud of having white skin and blue eyes. He was a Polish violinist, gentle and pacifist.

"I like them," I answered; "I like them because they're not like us. I'm tired of white faces."

"But they're nothing but monkeys, your Japanese! Clever little monkeys that steal fruit. They stole their religion from the Hindus, their art and culture from the Chinese and the Koreans, their science and technology from the whites. What have they invented? Nothing! They imitate everything. Yellow Americans? Not even that. Yellow monkeys!"

"Goethe said," I answered him laughing, " 'I eat pork and turn it into Goethe.' "

The white man sneered. "I once heard a hog bragging: 'I eat Goethe and I turn it into pork!' "

A young Japanese in white gloves distributed the day's bulletin: *The meteorological station in Tokyo reports that the* sakura *will begin blooming a little earlier this year, for this spring promises to be exceptionally warm.*

And below: *We shall be entering Japan's inland sea within the military zone. The taking of photographs is strictly forbidden.*

My poor pacifist interlocutor objected. "What's this?" he exclaimed. "All this *sakura* they boast about so much is just a mask? They only use it to camouflage the cannons and the oil dumps?"

"Didn't you know?" I answered him with a wicked delight. "But isn't all life—that other *sakura* we boast about so much —just a camouflage for death?"

Woe to the man who sees only the mask; woe to the man who sees only what is hidden beneath it! The only man with true vision sees at the same moment, and in a single flash, the beautiful mask and the dreadful face behind it.

Happy the man who, behind his forehead, creates this mask and this face in a synthesis still unknown to nature. He alone can play with dignity and grace the double flute of life and death.

The white man shook his blond head vaguely; he had understood nothing.

And I, I was happy listening to that distant double flute on the lips of Japan.

3

$\mathcal{A}$ GENTLE SPRING RAIN. My pilgrimage to far-away lands, burdened with the details of reality, evaporated in this tender atmosphere and assumed the feathery Buddhist consistency of dreams.

Japanese coolies rush to the boat—silent, short, squat, with muscular legs and burning eyes. They unload baggage, merchandise and passengers with a startling agility and strength.

Joshiro approached me, delighted. "How nimbly," she says in her harsh voice, "these Japanese coolies will someday empty Paris, London, and New York!"

The terrible vision burst upon me; it lasted only a second, but I had time to see the white man's cathedrals and stock exchanges and brothels ablaze.

"Don't be afraid!" the young woman said, laughing when she saw the glow of distant conflagrations in my eyes. "Look a little farther; give up your white man's prerogatives; it's our turn, it's up to the yellow race now. And it's a good thing; the earth has to be renewed! But let's forget about these gay reflections and disembark. We'll walk together through the city of Kobe I love so much; then I'll leave you. I have other places to stroll—and by myself."

Joshiro's face was radiant. We strode across the quays, took a long, ugly avenue filled with the sticky smoke of factories and entered the city: skyscrapers, shrieking radios, shameless movie stars, *mogas* and *mobos*—Americanized boys and girls, hesitant young people who were trying, despite their absurdity, to make a new synthesis.

Joshiro pointed. "In this luxurious hotel," she said sneering, "Rabindranath Tagore, that pudgy nightingale, one day complained about the industrial ugliness that was invading Japan. The poor man wanted an idyllic and cooing Japan, at the mercy of romantic tourists, and of your cannons!"

She shook her head, in a fit of laughter. I did not answer. I listened in silence to two voices that rose within me and argued: "How ugly! How this smoke dims the pure face of the geisha of nations! Soon there will no longer remain a single blooming branch left on the sad earth where that sacred bird, the human heart, can perch and sing!"

And the other voice replied, ironic and hissing: "Don't whimper so much, don't make yourself ridiculous opposing the inevitable. Try to find the austere beauty in the dry, straight lines, in the iron heart of the new reality. Make necessity your own will, if you would remain free in this world of slaves."

"Joshiro-san," I said, "soon the day will come when the old Japan—colored lanterns, kimonos, fans, geishas, *sakura*—will vanish from the face of the so-called Pacific Ocean. In a few years the old Japanese soul will slip on its most beautiful kimono, raise the high scaffolding of its lacquered hair and, in the twilight, at the hour when the radios begin screaming and the *mogas* are taking their cocktails with the *mobos*, she'll come sit down here on this street and commit hara-kiri. And you'll find written in red ink on her silk fan this melancholy *haiku*:

If you open my heart,
You will find inside
The three cords of the samisen—
Broken.

Joshiro began laughing; she gave me an ironic glance. "Let her commit hara-kiri then," she exclaimed, "and leave us in peace for once! The bow committed hara-kiri too, and broke into a thousand pieces before the rifle; the quill pen committed hara-kiri before the fountain pen. *Pff! Bric-a-brac!* Let her take her place in the glass case of an ethnological museum sprinkled with formaldehyde!"

Joshiro stopped talking for a moment. But rage boiled up in her again, unappeased. "We're tired of it!" she exclaimed again. "It's time to be through with that exotic carnival— kimonos, *sakura*, tea ceremony, sentimental *haikus!*"

I tried to calm her; I took her hand. But the furious *moga* rejected my caresses.

"You can't imagine, you tourists, what we've suffered in our old houses! We were hungry and we dared not eat; we spoke with our mouths pursed, laughing discreetly, hee, hee, hee! Like toothless old maids—*why?* To remain faithful to the sacrosanct traditions! Our faces had to be the shape of melons, and our poor knees were deformed because, from our earliest childhood, we were forced to carry our brothers and baby sisters on our backs. We didn't play games, we never had any sports, we never ate meat, and our skinny, wizened bodies looked like the dwarf trees of our gardens. Why? To obey the spirits of our ancestors! Isn't it better to obey the spirits of our descendants?"

Delighted and moved, I looked at my young companion. I no longer saw before me the smiling and timid eyes of the traditional young Japanese woman; in Joshiro's eyes flamed the first spark of a revolution on the march. They had certainly lost their exotic charm, but are the eyes of Japanese women made to please tourists? This *moga* who was striding

23

with firm steps through the streets of Kobe was the precursor of an irreverent and cruel generation.

I had the future of Japan beside me; I felt that this ingenuously audacious young woman was the most profound of all the philosophical and sociological essays on the new Japan. Everything she said or sought had an incalculable importance.

"You're taking a very dangerous path," I said. "You're pillaging all the white man's material progress; will you have the strength to keep your Japanese soul intact?"

Joshiro answered without hesitating, "We've begun, we're on the march, we must go forward. We must even go faster than the rest, in order to make up for lost time. How should we advance? On foot, riding on our oxen, in our rickshas? That would be ridiculous, futile. You white men have invented railroads, steamboats, airplanes—just in time! We'll use them. We'll devour everything, without shame and without scruple. We're going through the first stage of our development, which is deeply scarred by the sign of hunger. The problem of assimilation you raise will come later; we'll solve it then. For the moment, let's fulfill our first duty: let's eat! *Eat*—which means building factories, producing warships and cannons, organizing our material and psychic forces. Organizing Asia. All Asia—China, Indochina, India, the Moslems. Starting with China!"

At the word China, Joshiro's pale cheeks grew purple.

"But suppose Europe intervenes? Suppose America resists, suppose it's not in their interest, this emancipation of Asia, then what will you do? Make war?"

Joshiro frowned. Her face grew very serious. It was as if all Japan were weighing the pros and cons and were about to make a decision.

She raised her head and in a calm, austere voice replied: "Make war!"

I shuddered. I knew that the future was speaking through this young mouth.

Suddenly Joshiro stopped in front of a bar.

24

"Don't ask me any more questions!" she said imperiously. "Let's go in and have a cocktail."

We went into the bar. There was a lot of noise, an elegant bartender, flirting *mogas* and *mobos*. On the phonograph, a Japanese record. A strange, half-sad, half-ironic song.

"Would you translate that song for me?"

The moon rising now behind the skyscrapers—
Does it shine on the same love that it once lit up
When it rose over the plains of Tokyo?

"What's your answer, Joshiro-san?"

Joshiro laughed.

"The same old thing. To hell with love! It's always the same."

Suddenly her eyes grew stern.

"I wish I were a man!" she said. "Only a man can free himself completely, body and soul. A woman can't. Yes, our intelligence can free itself. Yes . . . yes. . . . But our heart, that naïve old muscle, still fights on with its poor, outdated weapons."

She lit a cigarette and her threatening face stared at me through the smoke.

4

$\mathcal{I}$ LEFT JOSHIRO reluctantly, the way one leaves a beautiful spring day.

"I'm afraid I won't see you again, Joshiro-san!" I said, suddenly filled with a rather absurd sentimentality.

"So?" Joshiro asked, squeezing my hand hard. "Live well, die well, control your heart!"

She knew that in Peking I would be Li-Te's guest; I stared deep into her eyes with a questioning look. Didn't she want to give me some message?

"Is that all, Joshiro-san?"

"Yes, that's all!"

I saw her vanish into the station, among the crowd.

"How strong she is!" I thought. "Strong and tender and inhumanly proud. Her vengeance may be terrible."

Suddenly I thought I saw the limping Chinese with the scar on his forehead in the crowd.

"What an odd coincidence!" I thought, but I paid no attention to it at the time.

I no longer thought of Joshiro or Li-Te, but of Japan and China. Love, hatred, vengeance; inexorable struggle; woe to the weakest!

The human soul is still burdened with substance, it can foretell nothing; it needs the body's eyes to see and ears to hear. I understood only later Joshiro's words and silences and the vengeance that she held between her little hands at the moment of our separation.

But I soon forgot everything, lured on by my vision of Japan. The dazzling spectacle exploded before me like an overripe pomegranate that splits in the sun.

Fantastic cities, Mediterranean beaches, men and women with bright-colored parasols, wooden temples polished by the caresses of the faithful, granite or silk lanterns, a strange murmur consisting of laughter, stifled tears and the deep sound of the giant old bells of monasteries. . . .

My body had to hear, see, touch, in order to believe in this Oriental mirage.

"Well! Brother Thomas," I often told it, laughing, "because of your incredulity you'll never enter the Kingdom of Heaven, only the kingdom of earth—and there you'll rot!"

"So what?" answered this valiant and sensuous comrade, "so what, as long as I see, touch, and smell before I rot!"

I opened my earthen eyes with a shudder of anxiety. I was plundering a Japan in bloom, cities and towns and summer gardens, and I emerged from it with my soul powdered with pollen.

Temples hidden among the trees suddenly rose out of the ground like furious dragons; and deep in their bowels glowed tender paintings, smiling statues, groves of delight.

A few vague shadows on a strip of silk suggested a whole landscape of hesitant and mystical beauty. Birds, trees, kings, women—all transformed and ennobled in the magical air of art! All the substance of their bodies expressed down to the smallest detail—but through the substance shines their es-

27

sence; more than their essence: the primordial music, the great Mother who engenders all things. . . .

The Japanese artist tenderly loves the form of things and respects it; but he loves still more the inner forces which, emerging from it and frozen for an instant, have given birth to this beloved form.

"Do not paint created things," instructs an old sage, "paint the forces that have created them!"

All these marvels of lines and colors lovingly interlaced in the empty air enchanted my incurably naïve senses. I often caught myself at the most touching moments of my delight reminding myself in a low voice: "Quick, open your eyes, before all this enchantment is scattered!"

Sometimes, toward evening, a shadow of sadness fell across my heart. Where did it come from? From the great depths of solitude, and I shuddered. But I soon controlled myself and mobilized all these beautiful things savored during the day—and the black shadow vanished.

In these brief moments of panic, the words of Abbé Mugnier came to my rescue. This "wakener of sleeping souls" had told me one day in Paris:

"Yesterday I went to see Bergson, who was sick; his legs were swollen. Imagine, the master of dancing thought—lame!

" 'Master,' I asked, 'can you give me the essence of your philosophy in a single word?'

"Bergson thought for a moment; then, in that caressing voice of his, he spoke the magic word:

" 'Mobilization!' "

I mobilized all my reserves of courage and joy and forced myself to transform each day's incoherent murmur into one clear note.

But all remained fragmentary, and the great spiral of joy had not yet swept up all the details into a creative cyclone.

Finally the day came.

I was at Nara, the sacred heart of Japan. I wandered into the park with its thousand deer, I followed the rows of moss-covered stone lanterns, looking for the old temple of the god of sacred dance, Kasuga. My heart was beating hard. For in this temple had been born Noh, daughter of the dance, the doe with velvet eyes, Japanese tragedy.

To make the spectacle of death a source of joy, to cast over the abyss a veil embroidered with red flowers interlacing bodies and fantastic gods, that is the most heroic and the noblest action man can achieve. Tragedy is the daughter of our proud soul which dares watch its own image vacillate over the abyss.

In the beginning, frenzied trance, chaotic emotions, savage cries. Man, abandoned to his demon, flings himself into frenzy. The monks of Kasuga danced wildly, in terrifying or comic masks; they wept and laughed, shaken by this sacred intoxication.

Gradually the soul in ebullition grows calm, the chaotic sentiments are subdued to a rhythm, the overflowing heart returns to its channel, then pours into the sea of divinity. Finally comes the Word, the great liberator; it gives coherence to the Cry, nobility to the extravagance of the senses. Life sublimates itself in art.

God, the only hero, fills the whole stage at first, and dances solemnly by himself. Men draw to the side and listen in silence to the devouring monologue.

God speaks in the desert of his omnipotence. He would crush man, a rebellious worm. But now man gradually raises his head. He takes an active part in the drama. He comments on God's words, he dares to answer his questions. He dares more: he asks his own questions. The dialogue between God and man begins, the action grows dramatic and is enriched. God is no longer alone, his sterile and monotonous monologue has ceased; man, finally, stands beside him.

Gradually he discards God; man assumes his first roles, which up till now God alone performed. Here, too, human progress follows the familiar rhythm:

One: Alone, God is sterile. Two: God and man, man and God collaborate, and the great civilizations appear on the earth. Three: At last man remains alone, and all civilizations fall back into the abyss.

Japan, in fitful, fertile moments of collaboration, has given birth to this superb, savage daughter Noh, the Japanese tragedy.

When I saw the old temple of creative dance between the trees at the far end of the row of stone lanterns, my heart leaped like a stag. I almost ran and reached the little wooden temple breathless, and thirsty, when I saw the spring that laughed before the entrance. I took the huge wooden spoon hanging beside it and greedily began drinking.

"Drink first!" I told myself. "First care for our poor 'brother, the ass,' the body."

The coolness of the water ran into me, down to my heels. I sat on a worm-eaten step of the temple and leaned against the column like a beggar. I stared deep into the gentle gloom: strange musical instruments, masks, sandals, silken girdles, fans. . . . *Koto*, the huge Japanese harp lying on the ground like a wild beast, was resting. Two girls, their hair spread out over their shoulders, were crouching in one corner, heads between their knees, like tired bacchantes.

I felt happy. How many years had I longed for this one moment! This wooden step where I was sitting was the goal of a deep desire. To see the cradle of a river or of an idea is always for me the source of an ineffable joy and sadness.

One of the two bacchantes spread her knees, raised her head and looked at me. Tragedy, with her long velvet eyes filled with sadness and sanctity! Those slanting eyes that stared at me, strange and motionless in the darkness, gave me the divine *frisson*: the same shudder that must have run through the bull when the high priest's knife brushed his back, from neck to tail.

We are the playthings of our fantastic imagination; a simple movement of the eyelids can unfold within us tremendous sleeping wings. I let that young girl sweep me into the motionless dance. I too plunged, into the heart of reality, the ferment of mind.

30

A little Shinto temple—the stage. A monk comes in, sings as he takes a few steps, and persuades us he is traveling. He stops. He raises his arms in an impulse of joy: he has achieved the goal of his long pilgrimage, the famous temple.

A second character enters: priest, fisherman or peasant. He exalts the sacred legend of the temple and the greatness of his god. Suddenly, mysteriously, he vanishes. It was a god, or else the ghost of an ascetic or of a warrior.

Alone, the monk begins his song again. A sad, monotonous incantation, a wild appeal; the plaint of a widowed woman. The soul summons its god.

The heavy curtain parts and on the threshold the god or demon of the temple appears in his true form. He walks forward, stiff, cataleptic, step by step, as if the whole length of his body were pushed forward by invisible forces. He begins dancing very slowly, solemn and impassive.

Terror seizes us. Man is overwhelmed; he dare not raise his head and look the demon in the face. The direct contemplation of the mystery would be unendurable to human senses. The soul would be seized with panic and no longer presume to live.

Then laughter intervenes. At the end of each tragedy appears—human, all too human, a little crude but salutary—Comedy: liberating Laughter. After each *Noh*, the *kyogen*, the "wild words," dash onto the stage, frolicking, laughing, to restore man's gregarious nature and make us forget the unforgettable.

The human heart is reassumed. It has trembled for a moment, leaning over the abyss; quickly it draws back onto *terra firma*, the gentle earth covered with grass and fruit. And it learns to love life with a desperate love; and it invents tender words to name earth, water, bread and woman.

The young bacchante turned away her gaze; I fell back onto the temple step, my eyes still dazzled.

I stood up and slowly followed a moss-grown path, listening to the litany of the pilgrims. I thought of God's passions that man makes into spectacles in order to comprehend and diminish his own agony. I thought of the unity of human and divine suffering, of the humble brotherhood of all things.

Buddha, Christ, Dionysos are all one—Man, the ephemeral, suffering god.

Step by step I followed those ragged barefoot pilgrims who sang so gaily as they advanced toward their god. Before us appeared a temple, a great courtyard, a row of cherry trees in bloom, bees that plundered them greedily. And at the far end, behind the sticks of burning incense, the colossal statue of Buddha.

I looked at the ecstatic eyes, the dry mouths, the shrunken throats humbly accustomed to hunger. They broke in mute waves upon the Buddha's knees and toenails.

And he, the great victor over imagination, the scorner of all consolation, gazed, his serpent's eyes smiling, at the human tide. His long hands multiplied in the temple's gloom, and each made a different gesture over these naïve heads: caressed, summoned, blessed, or threatened; clenched into a fist.

Sometimes I stared at Buddha, that terrible wheel in motion, sometimes at the pilgrims whose eyes, blinded by the light of faith, did not see the countless hands above them; and at my right temple, and at my left, I felt the two huge wings balanced.

Suddenly I was filled with joy. Staring fearless and disabused at Buddha's eyes, I thought I surprised a smile of complicity on his lips.

Suddenly I felt ready. The vague and perfidious music that wailed within me sharpened into distinct words that no longer let the meaning wander wide and vanish. My hands clenched with impatience.

I sat in the blue shadow of the temple and began following, under Buddha's ironic and paternal stare, the two lines within myself that pursue each other, interlace, separate and rejoin to make and unmake the Universe.

$\mathbf{5}$ *

W E COME *from a dark abyss, we end in a dark abyss, and we call the luminous interval life. As soon as we are born the return begins, at once the setting forth and the coming back; we die in every moment. Because of this many have cried out: The goal of life is death! But as soon as we are born we begin the struggle to create, to compose, to turn matter into life; we are born in every moment. Because of this many have cried out: The goal of ephemeral life is immortality! In the temporary living organism these two streams collide: (a) the ascent toward composition, toward life, toward immortality; (b) the descent toward decomposition, toward matter, toward death. Both streams well up from the depths of primordial essence. Life startles us at first; it seems somewhat beyond the law, somewhat contrary to nature, somewhat like a transitory counteraction to the*

---

* This chapter and other sections printed in italics, beginning on pages 52, 72, 114, 186, 201, 220 and 247, are translated by Kimon Friar and reprinted from The Saviors of God: Spiritual Exercises.

dark eternal fountains; but deeper down we feel that Life is itself without beginning, an indestructible force of the Universe. Both opposing forces are holy. It is our duty, therefore, to grasp that vision which can embrace and harmonize these two enormous, timeless, and indestructible forces, and with this vision to modulate our thinking and our action.

THE PREPARATION

FIRST DUTY

With clarity and quiet, I look upon the world and say: All that I see, hear, taste, smell, and touch are the creations of my mind.

The sun comes up and the sun goes down in my skull. Out of my temples the sun rises, and into the other the sun sets.

The stars shine in my brain; ideas, men, animals browse in my temporal head; songs and weeping fill the twisted shells of my ears and storm the air for a moment.

My brain blots out, and all, the heavens and the earth, vanish.

The mind shouts: "Only I exist!

"Deep in my subterranean cells my five senses labor; they weave and unweave space and time, joy and sorrow, matter and spirit.

"All swirl about me like a river, dancing and whirling; faces tumble like water, and chaos howls.

"But I, the Mind, continue to ascend patiently, manfully, sober in the vertigo. That I may not stumble and fall, I erect landmarks over this vertigo; I sling bridges, open roads, and build over the abyss.

"Struggling slowly, I move among the phenomena which I create, I distinguish between them for my convenience, I unite them with laws and yoke them to my heavy practical needs.

34

"I do not know whether behind appearances there lives and moves a secret essence superior to me. Nor do I ask; I do not care. I create phenomena in swarms, and paint with a full palette a gigantic and gaudy curtain before the abyss.

"This kingdom is my child, a transitory, a human work. But it's a solid work, nothing more solid exists, and only within its boundaries can I remain fruitful, happy, and at work.

"I am the worker of the abyss. I am the spectator of the abyss. I am both theory and practice. I am the law. Nothing beyond me exists."

To see and accept the boundaries of the human mind without vain rebellion, and in these severe limitations to work ceaselessly without protest—this is where man's first duty lies.

Build over the unsteady abyss, with manliness and austerity, the fully round and luminous arena of the mind where you may thresh and winnow the Universe like a lord of the land.

Distinguish clearly these bitter yet fertile human truths, flesh of our flesh, and admit them heroically: (a) the mind of man can perceive appearances only, and never the essence of things; (b) and not all appearances but only the appearances of matter; (c) and more narrowly still: not even these appearances of matter, but only relationships between them; (d) and these relationships are not real and independent of man, for even these are his creations; (e) and they are not the only ones humanly possible, but simply the most convenient for his practical and perceptive needs.

Within these limitations the mind is the legal and absolute monarch. No other power reigns within its kingdom.

I recognize these limitations, I accept them with resignation, bravery, and love, and I struggle at ease in their enclosure, as though I were free.

I subdue matter and force it to become my mind's good medium. I rejoice in plants, in animals, in man and in

35

gods, as though they were my children. I feel all the universe nestling about me and following me as though it were my own body.

In sudden dreadful moments a thought flashes through me: "This is all a cruel and futile game, without beginning, without end, without meaning." But again I yoke myself swiftly to the wheels of necessity, and all the Universe begins to revolve around me once more.

Discipline is the highest of all virtues. Only so may strength and desire be counterbalanced and the endeavors of man bear fruit.

This is how, with clarity and austerity, you may determine the omnipotence of the mind amid appearances and the incapacity of the mind beyond appearances—before you set out for salvation. You may not otherwise be saved.

SECOND DUTY

I will not accept boundaries; appearances cannot contain me; I choke! To bleed in this agony, and to live it profoundly, is the second duty.

The mind is patient and adjusts itself, it likes to play; but the heart grows savage and will not condescend to play; it stifles and rushes to tear apart the nets of necessity.

What is the value of subduing the earth, the waters, the air, of conquering space and time, of understanding what laws govern the mirages that rise from the burning deserts of the mind, their appearance and reappearance?

I have one longing only: to grasp what is hidden behind appearances, to ferret out that mystery which brings me to birth and then kills me, to discover if behind the visible and unceasing stream of the world an invisible and immutable presence is hiding.

If the mind cannot, if it was not made to attempt the heroic and desperate breach beyond frontiers, then if only the heart could!

Beyond! Beyond! Beyond! Beyond man I seek the invisible whip which strikes him and drives him into the struggle. I lie in ambush to find out what primordial face struggles beyond animals to imprint itself on the fleeting flesh by creating, smashing, and remolding innumerable masks. I struggle to make out beyond plants the first stumbling steps of the Invisible in the mud.

A command rings out within me: "Dig! What do you see?"

"Men and birds, water and stones."

"Dig deeper! What do you see?"

"Ideas and dreams, fantasies and lightning flashes!"

"Dig deeper! What do you see?"

"I see nothing! A mute Night, as thick as death. It must be death."

"Dig deeper!"

"Ah! I cannot penetrate the dark partition! I hear voices and weeping. I hear the flutter of wings on the other shore."

"Don't weep! Don't weep! They are not on the other shore. The voices, the weeping, and the wings are your own heart."

Beyond the mind, on the edge of the heart's holy precipice, I proceed, trembling. One foot grips the secure soil, the other gropes in the darkness above the abyss.

Behind all appearances, I divine a struggling essence. I want to merge with it.

I feel that behind appearances this struggling essence is also striving to merge with my heart. But the body stands between us and separates us. The mind stands between us and separates us.

What is my duty? To shatter the body, to rush and merge with the Invisible. To let the mind fall silent that I may hear the Invisible calling.

I walk on the rim of the abyss, and I tremble. Two voices contend within me.

The mind: "Why waste ourselves by pursuing the impossible? Within the holy enclosure of our five senses it is our duty to acknowledge the limitations of man."

But another voice within me—call it the Sixth

37

Power, call it the heart—resists and shouts: "No! No! Never acknowledge the limitations of man. Smash all boundaries! Deny whatever your eyes see. Die every moment, but say: 'Death does not exist.'"

The mind: "My eye is without hope or illusion and gazes on all things clearly. Life is a game, a performance given by the five actors of my body.

"I look on avidly, with inexpressible curiosity, but I am not like the naïve peasant to believe what I see, clambering on the stage to meddle with the blood-drenched comedy.

"I am the wonder-working fakir who sits unmoving at the crossroads of the senses and watches the world being born and destroyed, watches the mob as it surges and shouts in the multicolored paths of vanity.

"Heart, naïve heart, become serene, and surrender!"

But the heart leaps up and shouts: "I am the peasant who jumps on the stage to meddle with the course of the world!"

I don't keep checks and balances, I don't seek to adjust myself. I follow the deep throbbing of my heart.

I ask and ask again, beating on chaos: "Who plants us on this earth without asking our permission? Who uproots us from this earth without asking our permission?"

I am a weak, ephemeral creature made of mud and dream. But I feel all the powers of the Universe whirling within me.

Before they crush me, I want to open my eyes for a moment and to see them. I set my life no other purpose.

I want to find a single justification that I may live and bear this dreadful daily spectacle of disease, of ugliness, of injustice, of death.

I once set out from a dark point, the Womb, and now I proceed to another dark point, the Tomb. A power hurls me out of the dark pit and another power drags me irrevocably toward the dark pit.

I am not like the condemned man whose mind has

been deadened with drink. Stone sober, with a clear head, I stride along a narrow path between two cliffs.

And I strive to discover how to signal my companions before I die, how to give them a hand, how to spell out for them in time one complete word at least, to tell them what I think this procession is, and toward what we go. And how necessary it is for all of us together to put our steps and hearts in harmony.

To say in time a simple word to my companions, a password, like conspirators.

Yes, the purpose of Earth is not life, it is not man. Earth has existed without these, and it will live on without them. They are but the ephemeral sparks of its violent whirling.

Let us unite, let us hold each other tightly, let us merge our hearts, let us create—so long as the warmth of this earth endures, so long as no earthquakes, cataclysms, icebergs or comets come to destroy us—let us create for Earth a brain and a heart, let us give a human meaning to the superhuman struggle.

This anguish is our second duty.

THIRD DUTY

The mind adjusts itself. It wants to fill its dungeon, the skull, with great works, to engrave on the walls heroic mottoes, to paint on its shackles the wings of freedom.

The heart cannot adjust itself. Hands beat on the wall outside its dungeon, it listens to erotic cries that fill the air. Then, swollen with hope, the heart responds by rattling its chains; for a brief moment it believes that its chains have turned to wings.

But swiftly the heart falls wounded again, it loses all hope, and is gripped once more by the Great Fear.

The moment is ripe: leave the heart and the mind behind you, go forward, take the third step.

Free yourself from the simple complacency of the

mind that thinks to put all things in order and hopes to subdue phenomena. Free yourself from the terror of the heart that seeks and hopes to find the essence of things.

Conquer the last, the greatest temptation of all: Hope. This is the third duty.

We fight because we like fighting, we sing even though there is no ear to hear us. We work even though there is no master to pay us our wages when night falls. We do not work for others, we are the masters. This vineyard of earth is ours, our own flesh and blood.

We cultivate and prune it, we gather its grapes and tread them, we drink its wine, we sing and we weep, ideas and visions rise in our heads.

In what season of the vineyard has it fallen your lot to work? In the digging? In the vintage? In the feasting? All these are one.

I dig and rejoice in the grapes' entire cycle. I sing as I thirst and toil, drunk with the wine to come.

I hold the brimming wineglass and relive the toils of my grandfathers and great-grandfathers. The sweat of my labor runs down like a fountain from my tall, intoxicated brow.

Say farewell to all things at every moment. Fix your eyes slowly, passionately, on all things and say: "Never again!"

Look about you: All these bodies that you see shall rot. There is no salvation.

Look at them well: They live, work, love, hope. Look again: Nothing exists!

The generations of man rise from the earth and fall into the earth again.

Where are we going? Do not ask! Ascend, descend. There is no beginning and no end. Only this present moment exists, full of bitterness, full of sweetness, and I rejoice in it all.

Life is good and death is good; the earth is round

and firm in the experienced palms of my hands like the breast of a woman.

I surrender myself to everything. I love, I feel pain, I struggle. The world seems to me wider than the mind, my heart a dark and almighty mystery.

I am a sack filled with meat and bones, blood, sweat, and tears, desires and visions.

I revolve for a moment in air, I breathe, my heart beats, my mind glows, and suddenly the earth opens, and I vanish.

In my ephemeral backbone the two eternal streams rise and fall. In my vitals a man and woman embrace. They love and hate each other, they fight.

The man is smothering, and he cries out: "I am the shuttle that longs to tear apart the warp and woof, to leap out of the loom of necessity.

"To go beyond the law, to smash bodies, to conquer death. I am the Seed!"

And the other, profound voice, alluring and womanly, replies with serenity and surety: "I sit cross-legged on the ground and spread my roots deep under the tombs. Motionless, I receive the seed and nourish it. I am all milk and necessity.

"And I long to turn back, to descend into the beast, to descend even lower, into the tree, within the roots and the soil, and there never to move.

"I hold back the Spirit to enslave it, I won't let it escape, for I hate the flame which rises ever upward. I am the Womb!"

And I listen to the two voices; they are both mine; I rejoice in them and deny neither one. My heart is a dance of the five senses; my heart is a counterdance in denial of the five senses.

Innumerable powers, visible and invisible, rejoice and follow me when, fighting against the almighty current, I ascend with agony.

Innumerable powers, visible and invisible, are relieved and grow calm again when I descend and return to earth.

My heart streams on. I do not seek the beginning and the end of the world. I follow my heart's dread rhythm and plod on!

If you can, Spirit, rise up over the roaring waves and take in all the sea with an encircling glance. Hold the mind fast, don't let it be shaken. Then plunge suddenly into the waves once more and continue the struggle.

Our body is a ship that sails on deep blue waters. What is our goal? To be shipwrecked!

Because the Atlantic is a cataract, the new Earth exists only in the heart of man, and suddenly, in a silent whirlpool, you will sink into the cataract of death, you and the whole world's galleon.

Without hope, but with bravery, it is your duty to set your prow calmly toward the abyss. And to say: "Nothing exists!"

Nothing exists! Neither life nor death. I watch mind and matter hunting each other like two nonexistent erotic phantasms—merging, begetting, disappearing—and I say: "This is what I want!"

6

*T*HE AIR HAS changed its savor. By seizing in
words the vague music that roused my soul, I gave
the world a new face. Japan has assumed a fluid, unreal consistency that suits the needs of my spirit. I saw behind the
swarming, snarling and dangerous reality only the interplay
of earth, air, fire, water and spirit which compose and decompose Japan.

I had found in this intellectual adventure what I had put
into it. I raised out of the ocean a Japan with the countenance of my desire.

I required a reality with the apparatus of a dream in order
to put it at the service of my inner eye that saw the Universe
as a motley mirage.

The banana trees reflected there, the blue lakes and the
women have the same substance as the rainbow; the inner
eye knows this, but it delights all the same in the imaginary
banana palms that appease its real hunger, in the water
which slakes its thirst and in the women which suggest an
inexhaustible series of creative movements.

I saw men rush toward that morning mist, and I smiled complacently at their clumsy naïveté. I was proud and happy. "What is my duty?" I asked myself. To understand the great game. To take apart the doll of Earth, to discover in its belly the straw and the sawdust and the tiny ingenious mechanism that makes it germinate, bloom, fructify, die, and be reborn; to wind it up again without anger and without disgust, to watch it exhibit its marvels.

And not to be fooled by it!

Was it at Nara, at Kyoto, or else in the sublime mountains of Nikko? I was walking through a garden with great burgeoning trees, I passed through the red-painted Shinto gate, the "gate of happiness," I reached the wooden steps of the old temple dedicated to the spirits of the ancestors.

Not a statue, not an image that might impel the mind to restrain, to humanize nature. Nothing but a wide bronze vessel filled with clear water. The clouds pass over it, and you watch their reflections in the transparent water.

I leaned over and saw my own face floating there like a shadow. A leaf fell from a nearby tree and drifted across my face like a galley. A breeze blew and the water rippled, shuddering.

Divine nudity, naked woman, ephemeral happiness! My soul is filled with clear water like that bronze vessel on the threshold of the Shinto temple. Love, ideas, joys, horrible forebodings pass over it like hollow clouds and dead leaves.

Upon this Shinto water I contemplated, as it slowly passed, the severe, delicately chiseled countenance of Japan.

Later, in the imperial courtyard of Peking . . . A fine, gentle rain . . . I was with a young woman; we leaned over a pool of black water and I saw the two faces tremble, one beside the other, upon the dim waters. And suddenly I realized I loved that woman. For I had seen her beside me, upside down, in death.

Gazing into this Shinto water—was it at Nara, at Kyoto, or else at Nikko?—I realized one day that I loved Japan.

The trip had produced its fruit: a red apple filled with

ashes, and I loved it. It was exactly as I had so long desired it. I held it in my caressing hand as, in Byzantine mosaics, God holds a red orb, the earth; or as the lover seizes the firm breast of his beloved.

And now, upon the eve of my departure, caressing the fruit of my voyage, I took leave of all the joys I had experienced in these exotic lands and seas. With a secret delight I heard the glorious raven, my own nightingale, sing upon my left shoulder: *Nevermore!*

Nevermore! And my joy redoubled, that bitter taste provoked my pride, I wrested from death and bore far behind my eyelids, wind-beaten, rain-washed, the austere and smiling face of Japan.

Nevermore! I exclaimed, transported with delight. I am not afraid, I am free. Buddha has given me a sign, and we smiled together one afternoon at Nara, amid a blinding crowd.

"Nothing exists!" he had confided to me in a whisper. "Neither life nor death. Treat matter and spirit as loving phantoms that pursue each other, embrace and vanish, and say: 'This spectacle pleases me.'"

Thus I wandered over the abyss, the high ramparts of happiness, when I heard that harsh, muffled call that pierced my heart:

"*Help!*"

7

I LOOK ABOUT ME: a tiny garden, moist and warm; a stone lantern swathed in ivy; an old wooden bridge and the green water that flows murmuring beneath it. Three flowering cherry trees, mastered by a patient and skillful hand, bend like weeping willows over a pond filled with shadows.

And at the far end of the *sukiya* garden, the little temple of *Cha-no-yu*, the tea ceremony.

The hideously bitter taste of that hieratic tea still lingers on my lips. I see again the little bare room. Yellow matting. Yellow men and women crouching on the matting. Above me, hanging on the wall, a silk *kakemono*: the portrait of the grand master of *Cha-no-yu*, Rikyu, in his heavy samurai robe.

"Master, teach me the secret of your art!" an old lord implored one day.

"In winter, arrange the room so that it will seem warm; in summer, give it a look of coolness. Boil the tea suitably and give the tea a pleasant flavor."

"But, master, everyone knows these things!"

"When a man is born who not only knows these things but can also practice them, I shall sit at his feet and declare myself his disciple!"

I sat cross-legged at Rikyu's feet. Yes, master, you have revealed your secret; but it was so simple that no one has been able to grasp it.

The secret of the grand masters is like the secret of happiness: we expect ecstasies, lightning bolts, superhuman struggles, and yet this happiness is a very simple thing, very human, almost banal; God is neither an earthquake nor a conflagration nor a miracle; He is only a passing breeze.

A door opens noiselessly, a geisha appears sheathed in her heavy black kimono; she advances very slowly, stiff and impassive, like the priestess of a stern rite. She bows. Behind her, gentle and submissive, her knees slightly parted, trots her tiny companion; her smile is fixed like that of an archaic kore.

We hear the hissing of the boiling water. In the old days, bits of earth were put in the teapot, producing a strange melody; the guests listened, according to an old poet, "to a distant cascade in the mountains, the still more distant sea breaking upon the rocks, the rain rustling in the bamboo leaves, the pines murmuring in the wind . . ."

I listen; behind the thin screen of the bamboo wall, I hear the tremendous breath of Tokyo: a dim uproar of cries and laughs, factory whistles, automobile horns, and the clatter of tiny lacquered clogs.

"Master," I say to Rikyu, "forgive me, I must leave."

The little garden, crouching calm and discreet in a sunny corner of the city, exhales a blue mist, like a naked body. I breathe with it in the sun, and I feel happy to the marrow of my bones.

A *biku* in an orange gown, a wizened old monk with delicate hands, slowly caresses the rebellious branches of a young pine with an amorous and cruel insistence. His eyes never leave it, as if the pine were a beautiful and dangerous animal.

He tames it. Already the pine drags on the ground a long, green, intricate tail—like a peacock's.

In the humble routine of his mission—to master a tree— this old gardener follows the same inexorable and love-filled laws that the great ascetics have always followed, and he achieves the same arduous victory: he masters the rebellious forces of nature and gives them the form decreed by his mind.

I smile at this old gardener who has not lost the great secret of the struggle; I bow my head in respect.

He returns my smile; his hand, for a moment, remains in the air. With a little deferential gesture, he introduces the garden as if it were a great lord:

"It was composed by one of our old poets, three centuries ago. Can you understand, you who have come from the ocean, what it expresses?"

"I understand," I answer him humbly, "only what a Western barbarian can understand; little enough."

The monk laughs into his goat's beard; he is pleased. He crosses his delicate hands on his thin, hairy chest. His voice echoes, gentle as a song:

"Our old artists used to compose gardens the way you might compose a poem—a difficult, complex, very delicate task. Each garden must have its own particular meaning and suggest great abstract ideas: beatitude, innocence, solitude; or else pleasure, pride and greatness. And this meaning must correspond not to the soul of the owner, but to the vast soul of the ancestors, or better still, of his whole race. For, tell me, can the individual ever possess any value in himself?"

"No, indeed!" I exclaim, immediately conquered by this voice that is so determined and so gentle.

"The individual," he murmurs, "is a passing shadow; the garden, like any work of art, remains. It breathes eternity."

"What eternity?" But I didn't speak the words; I didn't want to interrupt the old gardener who was speaking in the name of a race of eternal ants.

"This little garden has its own particular meaning; it

48

suggests a great idea: solitude. The remoteness of human beings and their cares; tranquillity, the mute and resigned evanescence of things."

We are in the heart of an enormous city, full of noise and sin; we open this gate, we take a step, and we are deep in the green and mossy depths of solitude.

A little gate, one step, and we are saved.

The old monk in his orange robe gave me an amused ironic glance; he looked caressingly about this garden which was merely his soul made visible.

Suddenly he gave a start. He walked quickly toward the old bridge; a tiny moss-covered stone had been disturbed. He put it back in its place.

"Have you noticed," he asked me, out of breath, "how that stone destroyed the harmony of the whole? Some clumsy visitor must have moved it. One no longer felt the solitude, and the garden had lost its meaning; it was apparent that someone had passed; the spell was broken. Did you feel it?"

I didn't answer. My heart was saddened and humiliated; I had felt nothing. My Western skin was too thick.

I changed the subject. I pointed to the young pine that dragged its long emerald tail on the ground:

"How have you worked this miracle?"

"By patience and by love, very simply. From their birth, I caress, I force back, I solicit, I gently and pityingly insist. Every morning, every evening, I push the young branches where I want them to be . . . very simply."

I fell silent, embarrassed. This human ant walked effortlessly, without noticing it, on the heights to which we aspire with breathless ardor.

It is not he who walks, who speaks, who masters trees or ideas; over his thin shoulders and his tapering fingers I see the patient and countless race of the yellow man. In these profound countries where the dead dominate the living there is no individual, there is only the mass; and, above all, the terrible, impenetrable mass of the dead. Every yellow minute is heavy with centuries.

49

I ponder this gardener's method. And our inner gardens—love, cruelty, patience; to make our heart into a garden; to give this garden the unique meaning which can exalt our soul. To exalt and lead it with a firm step to death. . . .

I think of my soul . . . all my life was one desperate struggle with the powers of darkness and, above all, with the powers of light that each of us bears within himself. I struggle, panting, to reconquer at every moment what I have conquered all my life: that tiny arena of freedom, that wavering spark of the spirit, that unmastered, bloodstained, ephemeral flame of my heart.

Oh, if I could reach the calm peaks of effort and continue above the struggle without grimaces, without sweat covering my body!

"What are you thinking about?"

I raised my head; for a moment I had forgotten the old *biku*.

"I am thinking about the inner garden," I answered.

"O demon from the ocean, do not go too fast! Let us begin with the garden outside; let us train ourselves patiently, from step to step. Once we make a success of our outdoor gardening, we will start on the heart. That is more complicated, subtler. And afterwards . . ."

He hesitated a moment; he looked at me with a sadness mingled with compassion. And finally he made up his mind to speak: "And afterwards, we shall have to cultivate another garden. Still more difficult, more secret, infinitely superior, which contains neither trees, nor cool water, nor abstract ideas."

"Nothing but air?"

"Not even that."

"And what is the name of that garden?"

"Buddha!"

8

*B*UDDHA! The word fell, dim and sweet as a drop of honey. Never in my life had I enjoyed happiness so calm and so intense. "God is only a leap of the heart and a sweet tear"—that sentence of a Byzantine mystic slipped into my breast and filled it with certainty.

I was blissfully absorbed into the nothingness of God. An immutable and perfect beatitude. Was that immortal life? No one knows; but at that moment, in that garden of solitude, like an insect engulfed in the shadows, I felt myself immersed in motionless felicity.

And suddenly, at the most unexpected moment, immediately after the word "Buddha" spoken by the monk, that harsh and muffled cry pierced my heart: *"Help!"*

The monk had vanished. I leaned against the trunk of a cherry tree and bent my head on my breast.

Who cried out?

The cry echoed within me, from cavern to cavern, more and more dimly. Finally it grew silent again; it had returned to the inaccessible and mute sources of my being.

51

Everything was still now. My blood that had overflowed returned to its channels. I mustered my strength and slowly, laboriously, I set to work mastering by human and exact words my roaring anguish.

Who cried out?

Gather your strength and listen; the whole heart of man is a single outcry. Lean against your breast to hear it; someone is struggling and shouting within you.

It is your duty every moment, day and night, in joy or in sorrow, amid all daily necessities, to discern this Cry with vehemence or restraint, according to your nature, with laughter or with weeping, in action or in thought, striving to find out who is imperiled and cries out.

And how we may all be mobilized together to free him.

Amidst our greatest happiness someone within us cries out: "I am in pain! I want to escape your happiness! I am stifling!"

Amidst our deepest despair someone within us cries out: "I do not despair! I fight on! I grasp at your head, I unsheathe myself from your body, I detach myself from the earth, I cannot be contained in brains, in names, in deeds!"

Out of our most ample virtue someone rises up in despair and cries out: "Virtue is narrow, I cannot breathe! Paradise is small and cannot contain me! Your God resembles a man, I do not want him!"

I hear the savage cry, and I shudder. The agony that ascends within me composes itself, for the first time, into an integral human voice; it turns full face toward me and calls me clearly, with my own name, with the name of my father and my race.

This is the moment of greatest crisis. This is the signal for the March to begin. If you do not hear this Cry tearing at your entrails, do not set out.

Continue, with patience and submission, your sacred

military service in the first, second, and third rank of preparation.

And listen: In sleep, in an act of love or of creation, in a proud and disinterested act of yours, or in a profound despairing silence, you may suddenly hear the Cry and set forth.

Until that moment my heart streams on, it rises and falls with the Universe. But when I hear the Cry, my emotions and the Universe are divided into two camps.

Someone within me is in danger, he raises his hands and shouts: "Save me!" Someone within me climbs, stumbles, and shouts: "Help me!"

Which of the two eternal roads shall I choose? Suddenly I know that my whole life hangs on this decision—the life of the entire Universe.

Of the two, I choose the ascending path. Why? For no intelligible reason, without any certainty; I know how ineffectual the mind and all the small certainties of man can be in this moment of crisis.

I choose the ascending path because my heart drives me toward it. "Upward! Upward! Upward!" my heart shouts, and I follow it trustingly.

I feel this is what the dread primordial cry asks of me. I leap to its side. I cast in my lot with its own.

Someone within me is struggling to lift a great weight, to cast off the mind and flesh by overcoming habit, laziness, necessity.

I do not know from where he comes or where he goes. I clutch at his onward march in my ephemeral breast, I listen to his panting struggle, I shudder when I touch him.

Who is he? I prick up my ears. I set up various signs, I sniff the air. I ascend, groping upwards, panting and struggling. The dread and mystical March begins.

9

$\mathcal{M}$UFFLED FOOTSTEPS; a discreet cough. I turn around: my friend Kuge appears in this garden of solitude; his wistful smile gently brings me down to the Japanese earth.

I watched him approach, his feline body hesitating, his knees bent, his long thin arms dangling, his face pale except for his large, yellow teeth; but everything faded before the crepuscular gleam of his smile. I saw only his pale, smiling lips.

Is the famous Japanese smile nothing but a mask? Yet this mask renders communal life endurable, almost agreeable, and gives human relationships dignity and nobility. It teaches man to control himself, to keep his troubles and his pains to himself. Thus, gradually, the mask becomes a face, and what was originally nothing but a form is changed into substance.

"Kuge-san," I said to myself, looking at my friend. "Kuge-san, poor suffering heroic body, proud soul armed in a smile . . ."

Since the first days of my arrival in Tokyo, he had attached himself to me; I had met him in a temple—by chance, he maintained. He translated the inscriptions on the walls for me, he told me about the old sculptors, and in a low voice he sang the old popular songs.

I often met him in front of my hotel, by chance, he kept assuring me. We finally became friends. I was fond of him, for he was pure and ardent; his judgment was limited but sure, and his enthusiasm had the rare privilege of expressing itself in few gestures and few words.

A true Japanese, Kuge was utterly uninterested in metaphysical questions; he stubbornly confined his thoughts to the land of Japan, consisting of bones, ashes and the wishes of his ancestors. His sickly, nervous body, his eager and reserved heart found within the narrow circle of race every opportunity of achieving their highest, freest flowering.

Kuge trusted his heart. For that heart, he felt, was not an individual heart, a muscle that would beat a few moments and then stop; it was the eternal heart of his race. Kuge listened to it and obeyed; he knew that such a heart could never be deceived. That was why my friend's action was simple, sure and rapid.

"Oh, Kuge-san!" I exclaimed, delighted.

"Let us leave quickly!" he said in his low voice. "They are waiting for us."

I had forgotten about that tiresome visit to the great dynamo factory; I was not at all enthusiastic about it, but my friend Kuge insisted, out of national pride.

"You'll gape at the temples and the old statues of Buddha, and you haven't the slightest desire to glance at our modern temples, the factories, and at our modern Buddhas, the dynamos . . ."

His smile faded. He touched my arm lightly.

"You're leaving tomorrow, aren't you?"

There was something strange about his voice. Sadness? I turned, questioning my friend with my eyes. His lashes fluttered, but he smiled as if he wished to reassure me.

"All right, Kuge-san," I said. "Let's go now. You seem sad."

"Yes," he said simply, and smiled again.

How I have learned to love that smile, thanks to Kuge! We barbarians, we shriek, we cry out, we unbosom ourselves to our friends. We comfort ourselves a little, but by making ourselves importunate or absurd.

These heroic souls that burn in their yellow bodies have a disturbing charm. You feel that you've escaped your noisy village, Europe, and that beyond the white race lies another, deeper universe, more dangerous because it has more strength, more grace, more human dignity.

Ascetics and warriors, these yellow men see life as a field of honor, a passage of arms. Master your soul and your body, exert your will: the supreme good is not life, but beauty and honor.

These little Japanese have an implacable purpose: to create a new human type which has no fear of death; which, on the contrary, aspires to death as to the supreme crown of life. A Japanese general proclaimed to his troops during the Russo-Japanese War: "I do not send you to uncertain death, but to certain death!" And thus he roused the courage of his soldiers.

"The sword is the materialization of the Japanese soul," Admiral Togo once told President Roosevelt. Japanese steel, which can be bent into a circle without breaking. Suppleness, resistance, cruelty, the ineffable smile. . . .

On tiptoe, like a little fighting cock, the factory manager explained the complex marvels of its installations to us.

Kuge admired endlessly; he was very moved, he caressed the dynamos; his eyes slipped slowly, lovingly, over the beautiful gleaming machines. "Made in Japan! Made in Japan!" he kept exclaiming.

But already I felt an insurmountable boredom. I enjoy following the intellectual stratagems that have allowed man to master the forces of nature and put them at his service; I enjoy seeing man, in command of these all-powerful servants, transform matter. Beyond this point, it is exactly what interests the industrialists that leaves me cold.

So I looked away from the machines and watched the manager, who tirelessly ran about, checking everything, adding up figures.

He spoke of his factory with a strange respect and pride—as if it were really a superhuman being, terrible and benevolent, an ogress that devoured and spat out iron. . . . And this yellow Tom Thumb leaped about her, touched her with love and fear, attentive to her slightest whims.

Gradually I felt myself won over by the ardor of this passionate man; I began to understand that the fate of his enterprise was superior to his individual goals, his economic interests. There was a secret understanding between him and his race, and this gave the industrialist's rapacious ardor the sacred character of a passion that transcends the individual.

I went over to a pale young worker with blue circles under her eyes.

"Are you happy?" I asked her.

She turned her head and looked at me a moment. How thin she was, how sad and frightened! Her little black eyes signaled: "Save me!"

The manager furtively slipped beside us.

"Yes . . ." she murmured.

"Happy?" the manager exclaimed. "Of course she's happy. She's well paid."

"How much?"

"She eats at the factory cafeteria, she sleeps in our own clean, airy dormitories. Here are the figures. Would you like to make a note of them?"

"No," I answered. "But why is she so pale?"

The manager took my arm.

"Would you like a cup of tea?"

"Yes, yes. . . ." I was thinking as I followed the manager into his office, "The figures. . . . If I were a worker, I would write this bitter *haiku* in long black characters on the white comb in my hair:

Yes, yes, the figures show
Alas! that I am happy
But I grow paler every day
And this morning I began to cough. . . .

My wretched intellectual's anger was appeased by this *haiku*. The injustice committed against the human being had inspired these little lines, and I had almost forgotten the injustice.

I drank my tea and patiently listened to the manager's praise of his workers.

"The Japanese worker," he said, "is passionately fond of machinery. Every kind of apparatus attracts and delights him. He works enthusiastically, eight, ten, twelve hours a day, sometimes more, without fatigue. He's inspired by his love of machinery."

Finally I decided to be a little hard on this cunning and intelligent Tom Thumb.

"And you, the owners, profit thereby?"

The manager began laughing.

"But of course. You don't expect us to restrain this enthusiasm? My dear friend, we're businessmen and industrialists; we're not ideologists or ascetics!"

Each species has its own laws, and woe to him who transgresses or exchanges them for the laws of another species. If you give only grass to the tiger, it will die; if you give only meat to the lamb, it will die.

"But there are also humanitarian laws!"

"And we observe them! We house our workers, we feed them well, we see to it that they exercise, that their bodies are strong and supple . . ."

"So that they can produce more."

The manager laughed again. "Well of course! We combine the useful with the agreeable. Is that not perfection?"

I said nothing. The law of the jungle. Grass—poetry, disinterest, the lamb's sentimentality—did not suit his carnivore's organism.

58

Suddenly I wanted to open these predatory eyes:

"You're forgetting," I told him, "the great danger that threatens you."

"What danger?"

I dropped the word slowly: "Communism."

The manager shrugged.

"We've put it in prison," he said. "We've put that red bird in a cage."

"How can you put an idea in prison? It leaks out through the cracks around the doors and windows; it escapes clinging to the hair and the uniforms of its jailers . . . it spreads like a microbe, in the air we breathe, in the bread we eat, in the water we drink."

The industrialist was seized with a fit of laughter. "My friend, why don't you make a *haiku* out of that! Here, we swallow those microbes and by some Japanese miracle we manage to assimilate them and turn them into nationalism. Like the bees, we're able to turn a venomous flower into honey.

"But enough of these abstract ideas, they're no use. Action! Action! Take the British. When they feel threatened by the dangers of thinking, they hang up a heavy leather ball and begin battering it around; or they take their big curved sticks and begin chasing a wooden ball across a field; or else they fling themselves on a football and start kicking it furiously.

"That's how the English have got rid of abstract thought and look at them, they conquered the world!"

I stood up suddenly; I was choking to death.

Did the cunning Japanese understand my irritation and its causes? I don't know; but he half closed his cruel monkey's eyes and suddenly, in a weary, gentle voice, murmured: "As a matter of fact, action doesn't satisfy my soul; I hope you'll believe me—I'm eager to get home every evening. I take my bath, I put on my kimono, I go down barefoot into the garden. . . . I dig a little, I water the plants, I follow the progress of the leaves and the buds. I sit at the window and wait for the moon to rise. My wife knows how to play the *samisen*, and she sings some old poems. You know, they found the tender verses I like best in the helmet of the terrible warrior Taira Tantamori. My wife sings them marvelously: 'On my path, the twilight; the shadow of a tree will be my house tonight, and a flower my host.' "

He fell silent and looked at me, smiling.

I was delighted. What inspired intuition had led this fierce industrialist to understand that these were the only words which could seduce me?

After a sudden silence, he filled three tiny cups with warm sake and continued in the same tone:

"Our greatest poet today is a woman, Akiko. She has composed one *haiku* that greatly pleases me":

> *In the house humanity has built,*
> *Over thousands of years,*
> *I, too, add one gold nail.*

Half serious, half ironic, he added: "I've changed this *haiku* a little to make it my own":

> *In the house humanity has built,*
> *Over thousands of years,*
> *I install one dynamo—*
> *And produce electric light.*

10

*K*UGE-SAN, I'm glad we're alone for a minute.
You're a pure man, and I love you. You don't
exploit others, you don't seek material gains. You're deliciously uncontemporary; you belong to a mythical past and
also to a very remote future.

"For you, time isn't money, it's a precious essence, delicate, unforeseeable, full of mystery. Just to breathe with
someone like you, Kuge-san, does me good."

Kuge coughed lightly to conceal his embarrassment or his
laughter.

"Forgive me," I said to him, "if tonight, during this fare-
well dinner, I become a little sentimental. But tomorrow
I'm leaving for China, and I know I'll never see you again,
Kuge-san!"

The pretty Japanese girl who was serving us brought tiny
napkins that had been soaked in hot water. We carefully
wiped our faces and our hands that had been soiled by the
factory's greasy air. I poured the warm sake into our cups
and suddenly felt moved and happy.

"Watch out!" Kuge grinned. "Emotion is the first sign of old age. I don't like wet eyes."

"Neither do I," I answered, "but I don't like dry eyes much either; isn't there some intermediary stage?"

"To your health!" Kuge said, drinking his sake in one mouthful. "I don't know; let's try to discover or invent it tonight. Otherwise, I prefer dry eyes!"

"Tempura," the traditional fried food with bean sauce, and a lacquered bowl of exquisite soup, the tips of turtle flippers lying at the bottom.

To eat a meal with someone has always seemed to me a kind of communion—a mystical act, for all its ordinary appearances—which mysteriously unites souls. To eat bread, to drink wine with someone has always seemed a serious action to my prehistoric heart.

This evening I felt that this action was giving me absurd rights.

"Kuge-san," I said, breaking the silence, "have you ever been in love?"

My friend's face darkened.

"One never asks that question among us," he answered, concealing his irritation with difficulty.

"Nor among us!" I exclaimed, laughing. "But sometimes it's good to infringe the sacred code of etiquette. It makes you feel a little freer, a little more human. Don't you think so?"

"Etiquette," my friend replied, "is order, the august Mother of social life. I feel free in her talons."

He downed another cup of sake; his eyes gleamed. He looked at me ironically.

"O white demon," he said, grinning, "your face is already turned toward the West. You're leaving. According to your detestable white man's habit, you must have taken something of ours with you; surely you have found some treasure here that you've put in your pocket. Could you show it to me? I won't give you away."

"My friend Kuge-san, don't you know a man never travels except around the edges of his own soul? Or at best inside it?

At the ends of the earth, in the most exotic nations, you never find anything but your own image. From all the new things that dazzle our eyes and our minds, we unconsciously select those which correspond best to the needs and curiosity of our being, which is always concerned with its own interests and limits.

"Cold and asexual souls can perceive only what the camera lens sees, 'objective reality,' as it is called. But the others, male souls, female souls, which alone are capable of loving and suffering, come into fervent contact with landscapes, men and ideas, and choose ardently their loves and their hates."

"Right!" Kuge grumbled, and his eyes darkened.

I emptied a cup of sake to end my speech. But my mouth was still full of words; I wanted to get rid of them.

"You see, Kuge-san my friend, I'm not distinguishing between human beings as virtuous and vicious; nor as strong and weak, or beautiful and ugly, or intelligent and stupid; I'm distinguishing between them as warm and cold. All the warm people enter my Paradise, the cold go to my hell.

"The warm traveler creates the country he passes through. And he creates it, of course, in his own image. That is why, leaving your country, I have taken with me only myself.

"One day you taught me an old Japanese song. Everything I've told you is expressed in it with a precision and a grace that are truly Japanese. Do you remember it?

> On a twig of the blossoming plum tree,
> The nightingale was dreaming one night as the
>   snow was falling.
> And on the plain and the mountain
> There was nothing but snow
> Nothing but the rustling snow
> Nothing but the snow . . .
>
> One night when the snow was falling,
> The nightingale dreamed that the plum tree blos-
>   soms were opening.

And on the plain and the mountain
There was nothing but blossoms
Nothing but petals falling
Nothing but the petals of the plum tree blos-
    soms . . .

Kuge sighed ironically:

"Out of all you've heard, you remember only the poetry. If your head could be split open like a melon, there wouldn't be a single figure inside."

"That's what I meant, Kuge-san! That's what the song says. Out of all that confused muddle of words and actions, of all these incoherent spectacles that make up a journey, I've winnowed—I've made a selection. I reject what's of no use to me, I keep what's useful or agreeable, and with these little mosaic stones I compose the face of Japan. I mean: my own face reflected by a new mirror, Japan."

Kuge smiled with a touch of discreet irony.

"Then how do you see the face of Japan? That way we can find out how you imagine yourself. Or if my question embarrasses you, just tell me what Japan has taught you."

I thought for a moment. A cataract of colors, cries and odors exploded in my head—Japan. To choose, to reject, to select the essential!

"The treasure, as you call it, that I'm taking from Japan is expressed in a single Japanese word: *fudoshin!* Immobility of the heart. The soul's equilibrium in the face of joy and pain. Self-mastery. Knowing we have no right to degrade ourselves. For each of us bears on his shoulders the destinies of his race.

"The tragic sense of responsibility, that is the great Japanese lesson.

"I am not alone. I am not this ephemeral and miserable being I despise; I am a great eternal thing—my race. And I must always keep my heart unmoved, fearless, and without reproach, worthy of that great eternal thing.

"But Japan has also taught me a better lesson—I mean

one that conforms closer to the highest ambition of my being: Japan has taught me that danger and death can become a violent and very effective stimulant to action; and that one can pitch one's tent, without trembling, on a volcano.

"Not only pitch one's tent, but build one's house, take a wife, produce children on a volcano, carve statues of the gods, take a reed and write piercing little poems that fly swift as an arrow and lodge deep within the heart.

" 'The flower's color has faded—as I vainly contemplated —my face passing over the earth . . .' That is what your priestess Okono-Kumassi sang a thousand years ago.

"But that tragic notion of the ephemeral is violently transformed in the heroic soul of the Japanese. Instead of degenerating into sadness and fatalism, it becomes the inexhaustible thirst for seeing and enjoying, for accomplishing great actions quickly, before the earthquake, the volcano, the typhoon and death itself are upon us.

"That is why you have chosen as supreme symbols the rising sun, the chrysanthemum and the carp. The sun is your symbol of the three cardinal virtues: wisdom, kindness and bravery; the chrysanthemum resists the severest frosts and blooms even in the snow; and the carp swims upstream and conquers the terrible forces which seek to drive it down—as one of our masters of Western thought would say, the emblem of the ascending *élan vital* which rises against the current of matter.

"Japan is that heroic carp which swims upstream against the current of our descending, heavy age.

"These, my dear Kuge-san, are the two lessons which Japan has taught me; these are the treasures I take with me as I go."

11

$\mathcal{K}$UGE HAD LIT his long pipe and was staring through the window at the street aglow with lighted signs.

"Well?" I asked my friend, touching his arm.

Kuge turned around slowly. He seemed tired.

"You white men," he said, "you make everything complicated; your mind is an impossible ant heap. Japan is simpler. That's what is enigmatic for your white man's brain."

My friend Kuge poured out another cup of sake; he grew animated again.

"Let me give you a little example," he said. "As you know, Sadao Araki is a very impressive military figure among us today.

"In 1921, he was directing field maneuvers far from Tokyo. One day, he received an emergency dispatch: 'Your mother is dying and is asking for you.' Araki worshiped his old mother but he couldn't abandon his post at that moment.

He took a sheet of paper, drew Mount Fuji on it and sent it to his dying mother.

"Can you understand why?"

I thought for a moment:

"Yes," I answered, "but it would be too complicated; I prefer to hear the Japanese version."

Kuge smiled, pleased.

"Mount Fuji," he repeated, speaking very deliberately, "is the face of Japan, it is the severe and graceful profile. Fuji is our great ancestor which has molded our souls in its own image. Legends, gods, dragons, fairy tales, goblins, all the workings of the Japanese imagination live on this sacred mountain. Until 1868 no woman had ever corrupted its air with her breath.

"All the children of Japan have drawn the outline of Fuji in their notebooks countless times; it has taught them to draw simple, firm lines which combine strength with tenderness.

"Fuji has subjected Japanese hands to its rhythm and in any instance of our art, our life, you can follow the elegant and heroic line of Fuji's profile.

"The heart of Japan is not, as the song claims, the plum blossom; the heart of Japan is Mount Fuji, inextinguishable flame covered with immaculate snow.

"When Sadao Araki's old mother received her son's simple reply, she immediately understood that her son could not come to her, for he was kept away by duty. In the language of our soul, Fuji is the sacred ideogram that signifies duty. Now you know!"

My friend Kuge seemed excited. It was the first time he had ever talked so readily. Perhaps he had drunk too much sake this evening.

He controlled himself, bit his lips and gave me an almost hostile glance. He was ashamed of his excitement and resented me for it.

I closed my eyes a moment. I was leaving, saying farewell

67

to Japan. I thought of all I had seen and experienced in this land of the rising sun, the chrysanthemum and the carp. I tried to focus on the lines, the colors, the faces, the streets, the temples, all I could capture of this fugitive breath.

Japan with its old temples, their pools mirroring the clouds, its gardens gracefully wrought by the soul's demands, its whimsical décor of women and lanterns and masks, has taught me that the firm line and the free impulse do not exclude each other, and that we can desire and achieve the impossible without abandoning human frontiers; for these frontiers move and gradually retreat from century to century, before the pressure of human hearts.

If I could condense into a single image, into one suggestive thought my whole vision of Japan! In ten, in twenty years, what drop of all this outpouring of intense life will be spared? The motley lanterns and the spring dances of Kyoto, the temples and gardens of Nara, the pale, sad factory girl whose exhausted eyes called for help?

Or the omnivorous Buddha of Nara, that giant whose pitying heart and smile engulfed men, animals, plants and gods?

Great riches, disparate elements which cannot be contained in the "numberless monad" of the mind.

Tonight I had finally found the great synthesis: *Fuji*.

I closed my eyes a moment; for a few seconds I caressed my Japan in secret.

Suddenly I glanced at my friend Kuge and smiled. I was grateful to him, but dared not tell him so; his heart was a wild and prickly hedgehog.

I found him staring at me with a sadness tinged by hatred. What he felt for me must have been very complicated, and no word could have expressed it; moreover he must have changed at every moment, like the sea, or like fire.

I decided, that last evening, to startle him a little; to test his imperturbable and arrogant politeness.

"Kuge-san," I said to him point-blank, "you belong to the police, don't you? You're a schoolmaster in police service."

68

He blinked nervously but his face remained impassive.

"Yes," he answered in a low voice.

"So you've been afraid of me? Conspiracies, bombs, black or red watchwords, all that old noisy arsenal?"

"Yes, a little . . ."

"And now?"

"Oh!" he said, shrugging his shoulders a little scornfully.

"Oh what?"

"Now we know. A poet. A man who can be satisfied with words. Now you'll probably write some kind of melancholy poetry about Buddha. That's all right; you're on the right path, follow it. There's nothing to be afraid of."

A flood of rage and shame rose in my throat, broke over my temples; but I held myself back. There was neither idyl nor sentimental poetry in my soul; only a confused seething, a white-hot crucible ready to explode. . . .

Oh, the cowardly, poetic words that channel off rage! Shame, misery, rebellion . . . Someone inside me scornfully tramples me down, chokes and flings himself out of my soul to breathe a freer, purer air. . . .

But Kuge couldn't understand.

I looked up. "But Kuge-san, why have you come with me all this time, even this very last evening? You must have realized long ago . . ."

Kuge frowned.

"No . . ." he began, "you . . ."

"I what?"

"Nothing!" he said sharply.

I have always loved the oleander blossoms, for they bloom on a bitter plant. I understood my friend's irritation, his brusque tone, his blushes. He had felt a little friendship, a little tenderness for a member of a hated race. He couldn't forgive himself this weakness.

"How shall we finish our last evening?" I asked.

"Quite simply, by separating," Kuge answered, and stood up.

His face was a little paler than usual, a little harder.

69

"Will you write me once in a while?" I asked, laying my hand on his shoulder.

"What would be the use of it? Maybe . . ." he added, slipping away from my affectionate touch.

I held out my hand; he did not take it, but bowed three times in the Japanese manner, opened the door and vanished.

12

$\mathcal{I}$T WAS LATE when I returned to the hotel, a bitter taste in my mouth.

I spent a sleepless night in my room, my lips clenched tight. All the joys I had known in Japan were distilled already in one bitter essence. Kuge's word "poet" and his shrug of the shoulders made me blush with shame.

If only I could leave off this emasculating poetry of mine! Exorcise the fatal spell words have for me! Impose silence on that all-too-reasonable reason that mocks my ardor!

Someone within me struggles to drive back the limits. Tonight my body and my soul fill me with horror—I am choking to death. That evening, shaken by my contact with Japan, I began to discern the terrible face that screams within me—superior to me—and struggles for freedom.

At dawn I could bear no more; I made a new appeal to the detestable words in order to pour the overflow of my agony into them.

When I had finished writing, I felt a little relieved.

"Kuge-san!"

THE EGO

I am not good, I am not innocent, I am not serene. My happiness and unhappiness are both unbearable; I am full of inarticulate voices and darknesses; I wallow, all blood and tears, in this warm trough of my flesh.

I am afraid to talk. I adorn myself with false wings; I shout, I sing and I weep to drown out the inexorable cry of my heart.

I am not the light, I am the night; but a flame stabs through my entrails and consumes me. I am the night devoured by light.

Imperiled, moaning and staggering in darkness, I strive to shake myself free from sleep and to stand erect for a while, for as long as I can bear.

A small but undaunted breath within me struggles desperately to vanquish happiness, weariness, death.

I put my body through its paces like a war horse; I keep it lean, sturdy, prepared. I harden it and I pity it. I have no other steed.

I keep my brain wide awake, lucid, unmerciful. I unleash it to battle relentlessly so that, all light, it may devour the darkness of the flesh. I have no other workshop where I may transform darkness into light.

I keep my heart flaming, courageous, restless. I feel in my heart all commotions and all contradictions, the joys and sorrows of life. But I struggle to subdue them to a rhythm superior to that of the mind, harsher than that of my heart—to the ascending rhythm of the Universe.

The Cry within me is a call to arms. It shouts: "I, the Cry, am the Lord your God! I am not an asylum. I am not hope and a home. I am not the Father nor the Son nor the Holy Ghost. I am your General!

"You are not my slave, nor a plaything in my hands. You are not my friend, you are not my child. You are my comrade-in-arms!

"Hold courageously the passes which I entrusted to you; do not betray them. You are in duty bound, and you may act heroically by remaining at your own battle station.

"Love danger. What is most difficult? That is what I want! Which road should you take? The most craggy ascent! It is the one I also take: follow me!

"Learn to obey. Only he who obeys a rhythm superior to his own is free.

"Learn to command. Only he who can give commands may represent me here on earth.

"Love responsibility. Say: 'It is my duty, and mine alone, to save the earth. If it is not saved, then I alone am to blame.'

"Love each man according to his contribution in the struggle. Do not seek friends; seek comrades-in-arms.

"Be always restless, unsatisfied, unconforming. Whenever a habit becomes convenient, smash it! The greatest sin of all is satisfaction.

"Where are we going? Shall we ever win? What is the purpose of all this fighting? Be silent! Soldiers never question!"

I stoop and listen to this war cry within me. I begin to discern the face of my Leader, to distinguish his voice, to accept harsh commands with joy and terror.

Yes, yes, I am NOT nothing! A vaporous phosphorescence on a damp meadow, a miserable worm that crawls and loves, that shouts and talks about wings for an hour or two until his mouth is blocked with earth. The dark powers give no other answer.

But within me a deathless Cry, superior to me, continues to shout. For whether I want to or not, I am also, without doubt, a part of the visible and the invisible Universe. We are one. The powers which labor within me, the powers which goad me on to live, the powers which goad me on to die are, without doubt, its own powers also.

73

I am not a suspended, rootless thing in the world. I am earth of its earth and breath of its breath.

I am not alone in my fear, nor alone in my hope, nor alone in my shouting. A tremendous host, an onrush of the Universe fears, hopes, and shouts with me.

I am an improvised bridge, and when Someone passes over me, I crumble away behind him. A Combatant passes through me, eats my flesh and brain to open up roads, to free himself from me at last. It is not I but he who shouts.

THE RACE

The cry is not yours. It is not you talking, but innumerable ancestors talking with your mouth. It is not you who desire, but innumerable generations of descendants longing with your heart.

Your dead do not lie in the ground. They have become birds, trees, air. You sit under their shade, you are nourished by their flesh, you inhale their breathing. They have become ideas and passions, they determine your will and your actions.

Future generations do not move far from you in an uncertain time. They live, desire, and act in your loins and your heart.

In this lightning moment when you walk the earth, your first duty, by enlarging your ego, is to live through the endless march, both visible and invisible, of your own being.

You are not one; you are a body of troops. One of your faces lights up for a moment under the sun. Then suddenly it vanishes, and another, a younger one, lights up behind you.

The race of men from which you come is the huge body of the past, the present, and the future. It is the face itself; you are a passing expression. You are the shadow; it is the meat.

You are not free. Myriad invisible hands hold your hands and direct them. When you rise in anger, a great-

grandfather froths at your mouth; when you make love, an ancestral caveman growls with lust; when you sleep, tombs open in your memory till your skull brims with ghosts.

Your skull is a pit of blood round which the shades of the dead gather in myriad flocks to drink of you and be revived.

"Do not die that we may not die," the dead cry out within you. "We had no time to enjoy the women we desired; be in time, sleep with them! We had no time to turn our thoughts into deeds; turn them into deeds! We had no time to grasp and to crystallize the face of our hope; make it firm!

"Finish our work! Finish our work! All day and all night we come and go through your body, and we cry out. No, we have not gone, we have not detached ourselves from you, we have not descended into the earth. Deep in your entrails we continue the struggle. Deliver us!"

It is not enough to hear the tumult of ancestors within you. It is not enough to feel them battling at the threshold of your mind. All rush to clutch your warm brain and to climb once more into the light of day.

But you must choose with care whom to hurl down again into the chasms of your blood, and whom you shall permit to mount once more into the light and the earth.

Do not pity them. Keep vigil over the bottomless gulf of your heart, and choose. You shall say: "This shade is humble, dark, like a beast: send him away! This one is silent and flaming, more living than I: let him drink all my blood!"

Enlighten the dark blood of your ancestors, shape their cries into speech, purify their will, widen their narrow, unmerciful brows. This is your second duty.

For you are not only a slave. As soon as you were born, a new possibility was born with you, a free heartbeat stormed through the great sunless heart of your race.

Whether you would or not, you brought a new

rhythm, a new desire, a new idea, a fresh sorrow. Whether you would or not, you enriched your ancestral body.

Where are you going? How shall you confront life and death, virtue and fear? All the race takes refuge in your breast; it asks questions there and lies waiting in agony.

You have a great responsibility. You do not govern now only your own small, insignificant existence. You are a throw of the dice on which, for a moment, the entire fate of your race is gambled.

Everything you do reverberates throughout a thousand destinies. As you walk, you cut open and create that river bed into which the stream of your descendants shall enter and flow.

When you shake with fear, your terror branches out into innumerable generations, and you degrade innumerable souls before and behind you. When you rise to a valorous deed, all of your race rises with you and turns valorous.

"I am not alone! I am not alone!" Let this vision inflame you at every moment.

You are not a miserable and momentary body; behind your fleeting mask of clay, a thousand-year-old face lies in ambush. Your passions and your thoughts are older than your heart or brain.

Your invisible body is your dead ancestors and your unborn descendants. Your visible body is the living men, women, and children of your own race.

Only he has been freed from the inferno of his ego who feels deep pangs of hunger when a child of his race has nothing to eat, who feels his heart throbbing with joy when a man and a woman of his race embrace and kiss one another.

All these are limbs of your larger, visible body. You suffer and rejoice, scattered to the ends of the earth in a thousand bodies, blood of your blood.

Fight on behalf of your larger body just as you fight on behalf of your smaller body. Fight that all of your bodies may become strong, lean, prepared, that their minds may become enlightened, that their flaming, manly, and restless hearts may throb.

How can you become strong, enlightened, manly, if all these virtues do not storm throughout your entire larger body? How can you be saved unless all your blood is saved? If but one of your race is lost, he drags you down with him to destruction. A limb of your body and your mind rots.

Be deeply alive to this identity, not as theory, but as flesh and blood.

You are a leaf on the great tree of your race. Feel the earth mounting from dark roots and spreading out into branches and leaves.

What is your goal? To struggle and to cling firmly to a branch, either as a leaf or flower or fruit, so that within you the entire tree may move and breathe and be renewed.

Your first duty, in completing your service to your race, is to feel within you all your ancestors. Your second duty is to throw light on their onrush and to continue their work. Your third duty is to pass on to your son the great mandate to surpass you.

Agony within you! Someone is fighting to escape you, to tear himself away from your flesh, to be freed of you. A seed in your loins, a seed in your brains, does not want to remain with you any more. It cannot be contained in your entrails any longer; it fights for freedom.

"Father, I cannot be contained in your heart! I want to smash it and pass through! Father, I hate your body, I am ashamed to be glued to you, I want to leave you.

"You are nothing now but a sluggish horse, your feet can no longer follow the rhythm of my heart. I am in haste, Father. I shall dismount, I shall mount another body, and I shall leave you on the road."

And you, the father, rejoice to hear the contemptuous voice of your child. "All, all for my son!" you shout. "I am nothing. I am the Ape, he is the Man. I am the Man, he is the Son of Man!"

A power greater than you passes through you, smashing your body and mind, shouting: "Gamble the present and all things certain, gamble them for the future and all things uncertain!

"Hold nothing in reserve. I love danger! We may be lost, we may be saved. Do not ask. Place the whole world in the hands of danger every single moment. I, the seed of the unborn, eat at the entrails of your race, and I shout!"

13

$\mathcal{T}$ HE BLUE SEA, the salty air, a heroic breath. The invisible demons have fallen silent, the body's dear eye wanders, clear and greedy, over the waves and the gulls, and it is happy—for the world exists.

Toward evening, as we were leaving the last rocks of Japan, a dolphin leaped above the waves.

Its full, iridescent body, suddenly touched with a surpassing joy, took a somersault, to calm itself, gleamed a moment in a vibrant arc, and fell back into the water.

The earth disappeared behind us; with naïve anxiety I followed the death-agony of the mountains on the distant horizon.

"Never again! Never again!" I told myself, and Japan seemed to sink into the sea.

With saddened eyes, I looked around me. Chinese were heaped and intertwined like clusters of caterpillars on the deck. Blue cotton clothes, black-lacquered hair, women with mutilated feet, piercing, secretly hostile eyes. A pungent, heavy odor . . . shrill cries—an encampment of monkeys.

Something within me resisted, a mysterious racial aversion which narrowed and debased my heart. I felt unwilling to fraternize with this yellow swarm; I was ashamed. I realized I could not find the point inside myself where the two paths forked—the yellow, the white—and could not discern the trunk's integrity. My whole being repulsed this recognition of my brothers.

And yet I stayed on the deck for hours, fascinated. I could not look away from the malodorous mass that shrieked, laughed, and picked at its lice on the deck below.

The evening star appeared. The yellow bellies are hungry, the white rice is passed out in dirty pans. The chopsticks greedily snatch up the food, the ready mouths swallow it—insatiable, bottomless pits, into which the mouthfuls are thrown and vanish.

The pans are licked, the feeders stand up, breathe deeply. Some women nurse yellow bundles. Some men begin playing dice furiously. The Chinese bet their purses, their clothes, their wives; then they begin betting parts of their own bodies: fingers, ears. . . .

Opium, gambling, women—these are the three great gates of intoxication through which the Chinese soul escapes and wanders, free at last, far from the sordid realities.

A dreadfully emaciated old man, sitting cross-legged, opens a great book on his knees and begins to read aloud in a gasping voice. He sways back and forth, and the music of his words is unendurable and hallucinatory.

He must be chanting some scriptural verses, for the short women have crouched around him and the skeletal old men are in ecstasy. Gradually all of them begin swaying back and forth, accompanying the reader's nasal voice with a melodic murmur as if they were worker-bees, clustered, buzzing around the growing comb.

An irresistible and disturbing appeal draws me to this swarm of clammy flesh—a kind of vertigo. And somewhere in this disgust I find a doubtful touch of pleasure.

On the poop deck the yellow mass stirs, a space is cleared,

they crouch around it. A half-naked, muscular young man, his head shaved, stands in the middle of the circle. He begins to speak. He makes violent gestures, his voice is loud. He must be telling some popular legend. He acts out all the parts. Now his shrill, furious voice turns into the tender gasps of a woman weeping or making love. The audience bursts into laughter.

The tireless storyteller walks back and forth; he changes his voice, his gestures, his gait. He divides himself, becomes a man and a woman and a child. All the characters are there, miraculously detached from the actor's robust body. This body is a wheel of genesis turning in the twilight air and filling the circle on the poop deck with infinite presences.

The audience, men and women, is hanging on his lips. A frightened, naked child begins to cry; his mother slaps him, laughing.

I watched the inspired actor multiplying himself tenfold and I felt disturbed. I had before me a living example of the birth of tragedy. There was still only a single actor who had to incorporate all the passions of God and man within himself. The roles were not yet distributed among several bodies; one man bore the whole burden of destiny.

But how brilliantly! How consoling the function of art appeared, all smiles behind the cries and tears! A divine atmosphere of dreams emanated from this stocky, half-naked Chinese with his shaved head.

Now he was gleaming with sweat. A whiff of stench arose from these bodies excited by the show. I walked away, repelled and strangely stirred.

All my thoughts that evening were engrossed with the sources of tragedy. The man who experiences with such inexplicable intensity the griefs and joys which do not belong to him—the whole Universe—men, gods, animals, forces of nature—within him—he bears the Universe on his shoulders, like a head.

He smothers and begins to mime the passions to free himself of them; to cry out universal joys and griefs to keep his heart from breaking. . . .

The stage is set for him, he is surrounded by scenery. The motionless crowd, dazzled, opens its eyes and ears, feeling its heart swell until it can contain the Universe.

"The first steps," I tell myself, "of the creative dance, the first cries of the actor standing in the market place and calling to the crowd—what unique moments!"

Then I thought suddenly of the sources of the Rhône; how the river begins so humbly under the high glaciers and spreads undecided for a moment, then hollows its bed and descends roaring! Such, too, are the sources of the idea.

I fell asleep and then a "source," a spring, appeared to me in a dream: O Kuni, the beautiful dancer, the mother of the Kabuki theater.

I surprised her just as she was abandoning the Shinto temple in Kyoto where she danced for the gods. The complicated architecture of her lacquered hair was disturbed, rage broke her long brows; she fluttered her fan, suffocating.

O Kuni no longer wanted to dance in dark temples before impassive gods. She had conceived a longing to dance before men, who have eyes to admire, hands to applaud and warm lips to embrace.

I saw her hesitating as she descended the high steps of the temple and her delicate, nervous legs flashed as she came. Did they know, those legs, that they were taking the first steps on a triumphal way?

"O Kuni!" I exclaimed, able to contain my joy no longer.

She turned slowly, looked at me, understood the ardor of human desire and trembled. Her heart hardened; her ivory legs no longer hesitated. Yes, she would cease lavishing her charms on gods of wood and stone. Men! Men! Flesh like her own, warm, crying, ephemeral, voluptuously beaded with sweat!

She made a sign with her silk fan and smiled.

And for a long time, in the dream's heavy atmosphere, I stared after her as she entered the city, stopped in the great market place, uttered a cry of freedom, pushed up her silk kimono and began to perform her songs and dances.

O Kuni no longer danced the solemn religious dances; she danced like drunk men at fairs. She no longer sang hieratic hymns to the glory of God, but simple and daring songs to the glory of men and women. The fishermen, fruit sellers, artisans, peasants, women of the people and street boys surrounded her, amazed.

"Let me have no more gods!" she sang. "Let me have no more priests, the old priests without arms, mouths and hearts."

"Come, come, it is for you that I dance, O people!"

"O Kuni!" I exclaimed again in my sleep. "O source!"

Now she was following the dry bed of the river Kamo; she was dancing and the crowded shores uttered cries of desire. O Kuni was no longer alone; her lover, the handsome Nagoya Sansaburo, was with her; others too, men and women, a whole troupe.

Is not creation always a momentary loss of equilibrium to achieve yet a higher equilibrium, an act of madness?

O Kuni, the source, the spring, had refreshed my visible and my invisible soul all night long.

14

$\mathcal{I}$N THE MORNING, still steeped in this nocturnal joy, I made the acquaintance of an old Chinese, my table companion.

Kung Liang Ki seemed very subtle and ironic, the product of an old culture that had ennobled not only his mind but his almost transparent flesh as well—like the flesh of the silkworm toward the end of its evolution. . . .

Very obliging, very remote, his politeness was like an impenetrable armor that covered him, from the black silk skullcap to his feet. And when he made a more penetrating remark, he always accompanied it with a smile so affable that the edge was blunted and the wound was only a friendly scratch.

Kung Liang Ki knew my friend Li-Te's father.

"We're old friends," he told me. "We've both served the Empire; I, with resignation, abroad; he, with ardor and faith in Peking. More skeptical, more frivolous than he, I suspected we were seeing the end of the Empire, and I tried to enjoy the somewhat stale but still sweet pleasures that accompany all things when they are about to disappear. But my old friend Kung T'ang Hen was more ardent than I and attempted to change the course of the great river, to give destiny a face more in conformity with his own patriot's ambitions. He understood everything but he forgave nothing; the Empire has fallen, but he has never been willing to admit it. He has withdrawn into his house, sitting in the armchair of his ancestors, where he smokes his long pipe and stares into walls of opium smoke as he reorganizes the Celestial Empire."

Kung Liang Ki smiled maliciously. "He is fierce and taciturn," he added, "he is a great soul; he suffers neither the love of life nor the hatred of death. Be careful, dear foreigner! He does not like white men—but he is very polite."

That very evening I found the old mandarin dipping his hand into a bowl of water and slowly caressing a little jade marble.

"This," he explained to me with a smile, "is how skin can be made to retain its sensitivity. And you know how useful this sensitivity of touch is in life: love, statues, fruits, precious woods, silk, require a very delicate skin. Ideas too."

I ventured an indiscreet question: "How did you achieve that smile of yours, that is never disturbed by rage or boredom?"

The old man looked at me for a moment; he hesitated, as if he had a great secret to confide. Finally he made up his mind: "Do you know what the Tao is?"

"Yes."

"Can you define it?"

"No, I cannot. It penetrates everything. That is all I know."

"Then you know. He who can define it does not know the Tao. It exceeds all definition."

"Well?"

"Well, I have become one with the Tao. I have passed beyond the fugitive ecstasies that kindle us but leave us only black and smoking coals. I do not burn like a fire; I burn without exaltation and without failing—gently, like a little oil lamp."

"You have no fear?"

"Fear? Why? I am a free man."

I admired the race that could engender the stinking coolies swarming on deck and at the same time this refined and heroic being of such simplicity.

On the ship already chugging through a mud-colored sea as it neared Shanghai, I could see within a single glance the roots striking deep into the dung of China and at the same time the supreme flower that rises from it. And I began to understand the divine mission of the dung heap.

Stench and filth, by mysterious elaboration, have achieved, beyond an agreeable odor, the supreme form of their highest aspirations: the disappearance of all odor.

"Are you a Buddhist?" I asked again.

"Oh, you white men!" Kung Liang Ki said, laughing discreetly. "You always need to classify. You exist only insofar as you belong to someone or something. Your heads are filled with drawers and files. . . . Yes, I'm a Buddhist, a little. But I also revere Confucius, and I've always tried to follow his commandments, which are so deeply human. If you like, you can write on your file-card: *Kung Liang Ki. Religion: In his active years, Confucian; in his moments of contemplation, Buddhist. But active or contemplative, he has always regarded Buddha or Confucius as two masks that cover the same face: the Tao.*"

"But the Tao," I objected, "has no face!"

"Who told you so? The Tao can have everything—even a face."

"What face?"

"Mine, perhaps . . ." the old man answered in a low voice, and he said no more.

15

A MOIST TENDER DAWN. The silvery-gray sky smiled in the east, some gulls flew over us, elegant and ravenous. The Chinese on the deck stirred and ran about, emitting shrill cries like angry rats.

Kung Liang Ki, in his sky-blue silk robe, his round mandarin's cap and his black silk shoes, stood beside me at the bow.

We stared in silence at a fine and endless mud-colored line in the distance—China.

"China . . . China . . ." I murmured, and my heart leaped up.

When Mohammed visited one of his companions, the man's wife, the beautiful Zeineb, received him. At that moment a gust of wind parted Zeineb's robe; for an instant her firm breasts were revealed. Mohammed, dazzled and grateful, immediately forgot all the women he had ever loved and raised his hands to heaven.

"Allah!" he exclaimed. "I thank you for having given me a heart so inconstant!"

The moment I saw China, I immediately forgot all the countries I had ever loved, all my geographical *amours*, and began a new love affair with this land of Mongols' slanting eyes and cruel, mysterious, disturbing smiles. Let us thank Allah that our heart is so inconstant and that the wind blows and reveals for a moment China's eternally firm breasts!

The sun rises, the morning mists gradually dissolve, and China is revealed; green fields appear in the distance, the color of jade.

Just then I hear Kung Liang Ki's voice, frail and ironic: "At last we have reached the so-called Celestial Empire. But there is no empire in the world, Buddha be praised, that is more earthly. China is made of mud carried by its rivers and of the excrement of the living. Above all it is made of bodies —the hair, the flesh and the bones—of the ancestors. I wonder what a white man like you can understand of it."

"I did not come to your country to understand," I answered, annoyed by his smile and sarcastic tone. "I came to delight my five senses. I am not—Christ and Buddha be praised—a sociologist or a businessman or a tourist."

"Then what are you?"

"The ancient Greeks used to say that the soul is a 'co-exercise of the five senses.' I am such a soul. I am an animal with five tentacles that caresses the world. I do this to the best of my ability; that is why I fear neither irony nor disappointment. For me, China is a new pasture where I shall let my little flock graze, my five starving tigers: sight, hearing, taste, smell and touch."

I had not confessed the whole truth; I had hidden the anguish that drives me toward these distant lands. But I loathe effusions and easy fraternizations. Above all, I loathe the confessions that ease the heart. "Weep not!" exclaimed an old Arab poet to the sons of his race conquered in battle. "Weep not, lest your grief be lessened!"

This cry has long filled my life; jealously I keep my grief intact and powerful.

"Yes," Liang Ki said, winking, "but be careful, young man,

guard your little flock well. The Chinese dote on the tender flesh of such young tigers."

He laughed gently and greeted me with exquisite politeness.

"I have the agreeable premonition," he said, "that we shall see each other again in Peking. Be happy—and careful!"

Fleets of junks and sampans, with sails of rags and matting, pass like bats. High black, green, red poops; lacquered dragons, mouths wide, bend down from the top of the poop, and the whole sea is covered with demons.

We advance slowly through the muddy water. The port of Shanghai appears in the distance, forested with masts, decked with flags, humming faintly in the morning calm.

Necks craned, eyes squinting, we try to make out, just above the mud, the cursed city: Shanghai.

Several decades ago, Shanghai was a sleepy little port: a few fishermen's cabins, a few screams of anger and love; life here crawled on, patient and somnolent as the tortoise.

Suddenly the white demons from the sea fell upon this shore, bringing with them their terrible slaves, the machines. With a demoniac frenzy, they dredged the river mouth, drove piles, built their skyscrapers and factories, filled the air with a hideous racket of machines, sirens, boat whistles, shrieks on the floor of the stock exchange, and the music of the dance halls.

They brought with them that strange, perfumed worm-eaten apple, Civilization.

"China is beautiful!" I suddenly heard behind me.

I turned around; it was one of those white demons with hollow cheeks and anxious, faded blue eyes.

"China is beautiful," he repeated. "And Shanghai is its perfumed and starving mouth. Lucky the man who kisses her upon it!"

He smiled and winked at me like an accomplice.

"Women? Whisky? Dollars?" I asked, grinning.

The man shrugged his shoulders. "Not women, nor whisky, nor dollars. 'Chinese princesses.' That's what we call the handsome yellow boys with their graceful bodies. And at night, on the soft couches, the lights go out, the long pipes are lit and the screen falls—the screen the rest of you call reality. And the real world opens to us, the elect, and we enter into it . . ."

The blue eyes lit up for a moment, and then were immediately extinguished. The heavy jaw slackened and the mouth twisted. I felt the indignation and the disgust that the spectacle of decomposing human flesh and souls always inspires. . . .

I fixed my eyes, to refresh them a little, on the shore to my left where the last field glowed green; it was not yet—by what luck?—invaded by the Demons; it remained a tender green, glittering with dew, glittering with tears. Without realizing it, I held out my hand as if I wished to say farewell; on my return, perhaps, it would be swallowed up by concrete and steel.

"Let it go!" I murmured, suddenly annoyed. "This sensitivity among dragons has something unreal and ridiculous about it; this field resists, remains, rejoices not by its strengths but by chance, or by contempt. Let such poetry vanish!"

The poetry of the black dragons! The dry, haggard poetry of our times! Hammer out verses like steel! Establish harmony between the heart and the infernal mills. Armor-plate beauty! Find the heroic rhyme between our times and ourselves!

Perhaps Shanghai, the cursed city, is a modern poem. Woe to the man who does not understand it! Woe to me if I do not understand it!

16

*T*O SEE A CITY for the first time, to hear and touch it for the first time, to enter its streets, to make one's way down its lanes, to lose oneself deliciously in its alleys and byways, to smell its secret perfume, to explore its houses, its stones and its vermin, the human beings that nibble at it—what voluptuousness!

Only the slow penetration of a woman's intimacy can give even a pale idea of that voluptuousness which gives us pleasure to the point of pain. . . .

If such a prosaic and peaceful exposure gladdens our heart, what must be the delirious joy of the bloodstained conquerors who enter the besieged city that is finally conquered!

The ship puts out its gangplank and clings to Shanghai. Impatiently I leap onto the dock and dash into the streets that open before me in a motley fan.

Soon I leave behind me the pretentious neighborhoods of the white men, the broad, hideously straight avenues, the banks, office buildings and palaces, the Englishmen with the rare beefsteak cheeks, the tubercular Hindus who sell silk and tea.

I leave behind the astonishingly ugly churches, the municipal libraries, the hospitals, the charitable foundations, the whole clattering shopwindow of our hypocritical civilization and penetrate into the filthy swarm of the Chinese quarter.

"Be careful! Don't go into the Chinese quarter!" one old passenger urged me with a frightened look. "It's dangerous. Especially toward evening. You might end up with a rope around your neck."

Forget about reason and her old wives' tales! Flow with the tide into this yellow ocean!

I open my eyes and barely restrain a cry of joy. I never expected to see anything on earth so terrible and so alive. My joy rises in my throat. I feel I might be happier if I uttered a cry, if I seized the pigtails of the men scurrying past me or crouching at the street corners smoking their small-bowled pipes.

A strange intoxication impels us to dissolve ourselves into this viscous mask of countless heads. To surmount aversion and fear, to wallow voluptuously in this disgusting flux, to forget where we came from and where we are going . . .

A yellow Dionysos with slanting eyes, infinitely more troubling and more profound than the other, pours out a heady lotus wine.

Gradually the intoxication subsides and I begin to see clearly. Tiny flag-decked streets, signs with amazing carved wood dragons and fantastic birds, tiny cell-like shops where little yellow bodies, bent double, patiently work iron, ivory and leather; their hands, guided by thousands of invisible ancestors' hands, make traditional gestures of an impeccable skill. Others light fires, cook, eat greedily, mouths glued to the pans.

Women in long blue or black trousers, sitting cross-legged on the ground, nurse their offspring. Others scurry on their mutilated feet, swaying their enormous hips. Men crouching in a row comfort each other by chatting calmly.

Here each human being is a cloaca; countless is the filth that he heaps up as he passes, over thousands of years; that is how this thick, elastic and fecund rind of China has been formed.

A hideous smell; the air is sticky, it clings to the nostrils.

"Patience, my heart! Patience," I murmured, holding my nose. "This is the Orient. Try, if you can, to take the secret path followed by those huge Oriental oysters that transform their sickness into one great pearl."

Lepers with rotting fingers sell watermelon seeds and rice cakes. A hairdresser, one cheek ravaged by eczema, trims the beard of an old coolie on the sidewalk at the street corner; a fat prostitute with paper flowers in her scanty hair shrieks at the passers-by.

I walk slowly, trying not to be overcome by my panic; I want to enjoy this terrible spectacle without fainting away.

You cross the streets of Shanghai and you shudder, as if you had suddenly fallen into the jungle. The faces are strained, pitiless, on the prowl. Eyes are full of savagery and haste. The white men run, climb stairs, open doors lean over desks, clench their teeth writing figures, make telephone calls, send urgent messages, do business.

Insatiable thirst for gold, panting voluptuousness, the terrible instincts of hunger, love exasperated to the point of panic. For the white men, the insolent masters, are being pursued. All around them rises the Chinese wall of hatred. And the wall closes in, a little more every day, like a noose. Countless little eyes, slanting and voracious, watch the white men and lie in wait.

Sooner or later, the great day will come. It is approaching step by step. The Chinese press their ears to the ground and hear it coming. Sometimes with muffled footsteps, sometimes with noisy cries: "Drive the white men into the sea!"

Evening falls. Night follows, the great accomplice. The banks, offices and shops close. The white men stretch and yawn, stand up, perfume themselves and go out into the streets. They were wolves during the day; at night they turn into pigs.

The paper lanterns are lit; red with black dragons, green with orchid blossoms. Fu Chow, the great street of gaiety, gleams with motley lights. Savage and irresistible, the jazz screams out its first cries.

Those nocturnal peacocks the prostitutes awaken. They make their rounds, preening their feathers one by one, putting on their make-up; the silent coolies prostrate themselves, the whores get into their velvet rickshas. For a moment, as they raise their foot, one leg and thigh gleam suddenly through the split in the dress. Others stride boldly through the streets like yellow archangels.

They are all in a hurry. They go from one cabaret to the other, from restaurant to restaurant, they sing a little, they smile, they caress men like sick children; again their leg gleams like steel, they get back into their rickshas, impassive and a little sad, and hurry toward other clients.

Their hair is a little mussed, their lipstick gradually fades. They take out a tiny mirror, rearrange the fringe that covers their foreheads, reapply the lipstick and continue their march through the night.

Midnight. I cannot bring myself to go to bed. I wander through the streets, eyes wide, ears cocked, sliding along the housefronts like a spy.

Square courtyards, three or four dilapidated stories, a few twinkling lights. A row of doors all around, like a cloister. But these are not cloisters: from the top of the balustrade, half-naked women lean down and call. A stale smell of perfumed soap and *eau de Cologne* . . . a window opens, someone's bath water is poured down, sudden cries, laughter, then the window closes again and once more everything subsides to the suspect silence. And the half-naked bodies reappear on the balustrade and call in their harsh voices.

In these great market places of flesh, sexual stores, you can see, for a few dollars, "all that can happen in a bedroom," all the ignominies and miseries and horrors of lust. And you are disgusted forever (if you have a soul) with man and with woman.

Shanghai has an infernal greatness. It is beyond life and death. It is feverish, hurrying to profit and to enjoy, obsessed by forebodings, and awaits the dawn in anguish.

In Colombo, in Singapore, the white man's vile bondage is not so degrading and not so morose. Heat, humidity paralyze the tropical trees and the torpor invades you; you enter Nirvana, and you voluptuously dissolve into the great All. You become tree, cloud, shadow of the tree and of the cloud; you cease to exist.

But you cease to exist by identifying yourself with something superior to you, something immense, something eternal. You do not degrade yourself, you become divine.

Here in Shanghai, you degrade yourself. You lose yourself by dwindling to something lower than yourself, something narrower, something beneath the human soul.

Yes, Shanghai is a sublime and cursed city. It moves on, prophesying the form our exhausted world is soon to take. It is the monstrous flower of culture, with iron stamens and a rotten heart. Such must have been Nineveh and Babylon, Egyptian Thebes and Cretan Knossos when they were ripe at last—shameless, incredulous, disgorging wealth and wit, ready to die.

A little after midnight I cross the lobby of a huge, illuminated building. In it people are playing mah-jongg, fantan, roulette; people eat, dance, smoke, make love. Beautiful Chinese girls, slender, greedy, unsatisfied, gamble away their jewels and their bodies; generals squander the pay of their soldiers; students their tiny greedy youth.

I wander, lost, in this yellow hell and smell the harsh odor of beautiful sweating bodies.

"We're living at last—about time! We didn't choose the day of our birth. So now we'll celebrate the end with all the intensity of bodies and souls that have no tomorrow!"

A door opens, shrieks of joy, laughter, the rattle of swords —a woman's voice, drunk and raucous.

I shudder; where have I heard that voice before?

The door was half open; waiters with stern faces pass in and out carrying huge trays and tall bottles.

Now the woman has begun to sing: her rasping, throaty voice had a savage thrill about it. It was no longer a human voice; it was the frenzied call of a tigress in heat.

I craned my neck, trying to see. Who was this woman? A hideous suspicion had flashed through my mind, but I dared not face it.

An arm shot out and barred my way. I looked up. The mysterious Chinese with the scar stood before me.

I stepped back with a shudder and dashed out of that infernal house, my heart in my throat.

"Why? Why?" I stammered, stunned with inexplicable grief. "Why has Joshiro come to this?"

17

I GET INTO a ricksha and happily reread the telegram from my friend Li-Te in Peking. "Father, sister and I eagerly await your visit to our house with delight. Come soon."

A figure appears in my memory, slender, elegant, sober—my friend Li-Te. Our years at Oxford, the uncertain, alluring opportunities on the threshold of the future, the charming insolence of youth.

Li-Te loved flowers, women and boxing. He was taciturn and passionate. People were afraid of his smile. A legend of cold cruelty cut him off from others. But we had become friends; in me he saw a man struggling desperately to transform his bestial instincts into clear thoughts, and this struggle attracted him. In him I saw a dangerous and cunning leopard who delighted in human flesh but was holding himself back; at every moment he was transforming his hunger into smiles.

We were both tremendously repressed; under the human

mask we scrupulously concealed two wild beasts—Li-Te on the level of action, I on the even fiercer level of contemplation.

"We are two halves," I told him one day. "Two stumps of a great soul. Two mutilated beings."

As was his hideous habit, Li-Te ground his teeth and did not answer. But that evening he grinned, and his great white teeth gleamed threateningly. "I hate ideas, dreams and masturbation. Only the rage that turns itself into action pleases me—Genghis Khan!"

The steppes of Central Asia suddenly opened, at these words, and invaded Oxford. The Tartar Khan with his red hair, his blue-fox fur, his white charger.

"What is the greatest joy man can achieve?" Genghis Khan asks his companions one day.

"To return from war victorious and sit in his garden, listening to the chatter of his wives . . ."

"No!" Genghis Khan exclaims. "No! To dance upon his enemy's body!"

Li-Te looked at me, smiling.

"What are you thinking about?" he asked me.

"Genghis Khan."

Li-Te frowned.

"Why?" he asked, annoyed. "It's my job to think about the wolf. You should be thinking of your Jesus Christ, the lamb!"

My ricksha boy stopped. I returned quickly to Shanghai. The coolie pointed to a woman shouting from a roof.

I looked up, intrigued. A fat, disheveled woman was running back and forth along the low roof of her whitewashed mud hut. She was shouting and shaking her fist at the people in the street. There was foam around her wide lips.

"What's the matter with her?" I asked my coolie.

"Ch'i," he answered with indifference. "Black rage; she's insulting the street."

"Why?"

"She can't stand any more; she's choking, that's all!"

A strange shudder ran down my spine. That was *ch'i*, the black fury, the "sacred malady" of the race.

The madwoman flung herself around on her roof, she tore her blue cotton pajamas, her harsh voice sounded like a death rattle. From time to time she stopped and flung open her fan; she fanned herself furiously.

That is how the Chinese are occasionally seized by the demon. They are calm, placid, they smile, delouse themselves, smoke. They kill themselves at work, on land as on water, without complaining. But suddenly the demon falls upon them. They climb to the roofs and they insult the street; they go down into the street, noose in hand. Furiously they commit murder or suicide. The excessive and impotent rage strikes them down.

Queen Lu, twenty centuries ago, was patient and gentle. But suddenly foam covered her royal lips. She cut off the hands and feet of the king's concubine, the beautiful Tse. She put out her eyes, cut off her ears, and poured molten lead down her throat. Then, taking her in her arms, she hurled her into the cistern and began dancing upon her body.

The Chinese stores up everything, and nothing escapes him. He inscribes the tiniest amounts in your debit column. And one day, certainly, you will pay it.

"Quick!" I shouted to my coolie, who was sitting on the ground resting and smoking. He calmly stuck his pipe in his belt and began running toward the station.

"Today my day has not been wasted!" I thought. "I've seen that Chinese woman; bless her. She's given me a glimpse of the terrible China that has begun walking East."

I had a start of fear: "What if one day the *ch'i* seizes not only a single Chinese woman but all of China itself?

Here and there, rehearsals have occurred. One day in 1900 dreadful cries echoed in the streets of Peking, and it was no longer a single actress, a Chinese woman, but a whole troupe.

"Kill the white men! Drive them into the sea!"

Furious prophets ran through the streets, rousing the rabble. "The white men insult our gods, and the rain refuses to fall on our fields. Rise up, countrymen! Eight million spirits will descend from heaven and come to our aid! Unite with them! Kill the white men! Throw them into the sea!"

How can a man be made to struggle for freedom without an appeal to his deepest instincts? Hatred, hunger, thirst and revenge are tremendous powers that must be mobilized. The virtues, bourgeois or not, are insufficient to shake off man's torpor.

On that day, some thousands of coolies, the Yi Ho Tuan, the Boxers, were seized with their black rage. They ran through the streets like demons. The savage faith increased their strength tenfold.

Miracles occurred. Long nails were driven into these prophets, knives were thrust into their flesh without a single drop of blood being shed. Sacred fasts were proclaimed. Religious hymns were intoned, proclamations with vehement exhortations written on them were burned and their ashes devoured. People climbed trees and leaped from rooftops, foaming lips hissed with confused and bloody oracles.

One fanatic cut up his young daughter and threw the pieces to the faithful. The heads of the fanatics were wrapped around with turbans on which was written the word *Fu*: happiness. They stormed into the official district but the rifles, cannon and grenades that decimated them could not stop their fury.

This fit of *ch'i* lasted three months. Then the coolies subsided, their fever fell, they resumed their humble labors and began bowing again to the white lords. Again they were silent, smiling, repressing their black rage—until their souls gradually filled with it again.

My coolie stopped. "The station," he said, and greedily thrust out his hand.

I began counting out the heavy brass coins. The palm of his hand was filled with pennies, he emptied it into his pocket and held it out again.

A passing Englishman stopped and watched us.

I began to fill the coolie's hand again.

Suddenly the Englishman strode over and kicked the coolie hard in the belly; he shouted a few words at him in Chinese.

Some thirty Chinese clustered around us and watched, motionless and mute.

"You gave him too much!" the Englishman, his voice harsh with reproach, told me. "You mustn't spoil them."

I began laughing. "It doesn't matter! I feel sorry for him!"

"You mustn't!" the Englishman answered dryly. "You mustn't! You're in China, don't forget it!"

"But then why didn't you just tell me, instead of kicking him like that?"

"He'd begin to whine. The kick frightened him. It's the only way."

I went into the station.

The only way! Four hundred and fifty million Chinese on one side, and one Englishman on the other. But for how long?

I glanced back at the Chinese who had clustered around us. Not one had moved his lips, had flickered his eyelids. Their faces had remained as motionless as masks. Their fists were clenched.

The Chinese stores up rage, collects insults and ridicule. And one day his heart will overflow. Will the fleets of demons from across the sea have time to save so many white throats on that day?

18

I SHALL NEVER forget that evening, the fifth after I left Shanghai.

I was going up toward Peking, zigzagging across the immense landscape of China. From the first, the sober and majestic landscape had conquered me. I never tired of admiring, with a kind of holy terror, the Yangtse, the broad artery that nourishes and so often swallows up millions of souls like a true Oriental ogre—god of life and death.

It is a dragon that licks up bamboos and villages, floods the rice fields, receives all the garbage and slowly descends to the sea, carrying blue corpses and enormous masses of mud.

That night its scales gleamed in the pale light of the full moon. Its thick waters lapped at the side of an old boat garlanded with mauve-flowered climbing plants. Strange gurgles and little shrieks of rodents or excited women came from this boat moored to the bank.

Old matting on the deck, little cushions scattered about,

the pungent smell of opium, eyes which flashed in the half darkness with yellow flames like wild creatures surprised. On either side, motionless and mute, lay the musky courtesans, the yellow sirens.

Their painted lips bled like wounds, their cheeks were the "color of drunkenness," their eyebrows were shaved and above them had been painted very slender divergent antennae, "like the silhouette of distant mountains."

I had noticed them as soon as I stepped onto the deck and I shuddered as though I were standing in front of a tangle of gigantic vipers.

Gradually my eyes grew accustomed to the half darkness, and crouching behind these painted idols I made out several dozen skinny Chinese smoking opium pipes, their eyes lost in the distance. They never looked at the women, only stared across the water, which was now carrying away the moon, following their faceless dream.

The spangles, the jade, the earrings, the bronze bracelets sparkled suddenly in the moonlight. The river breathed like a nocturnal animal and the boat moved gently with its powerful breathing.

This barge of love drifting on the muddy stream seemed like the floating cathedral of an eternal religion. It was filled with saints and martyrs stretched out on the matting, heads surrounded by a phosphorescent halo.

On their hospitable and heroic breasts gleamed the ex-votos offered by the faithful: gold trinkets, jade pendants, deep bites, cigarette burns. . . .

The stars glittered like crystal over their heads, and in the musky darkness silent rites were being performed—the age-old gestures of arms that open, hands that grope. . . .

I walked past slowly and tried, by moonlight, to discover one human face among these identical and spectral apparitions. Suddenly I longed to crouch humbly beside one of these creatures.

A gentle compassion had overcome me, an unexpected impulse of sacrifice, the sudden revelation of my leprous brothers and sisters.

And then the sacred Acropolis I loved so much rose gently into the air. In spring, the green valley of Umbria, the flowering hawthorn hedges, the dark girls with their huge eyes who sit in the doorways making lace, a white dove cooing among the monastery bells . . .

The silvery voice of the playful bells of Santa Chiara that halts and then resumes its mock runaway—it stops again and waits. And then, at last, the tremendous sound of the great bell of the monastery of St. Francis, deep, male and ardent, which drowns out the elegant little bell of the nearby saint.

For a second Santa Chiara falls silent, astonished, but soon she musters her strength and peals out her silvery cries again, laughing, heedless, intoxicated with happiness . . . and the two voices mingle in the air, uniting like two bodies.

Enchanted, I followed the sound of the bells through the steep little streets and plunged into the cool darkness of the Poverello's church. And gradually the springlike frescoes of Giotto begin to flower in the gloom. The paintings gradually come into being, like Proserpina, fresh as the dawn, her rosy fingers parting the Byzantine shroud.

Love, purity, spring! The risen Christ stepping on the young grass, and the grass not bending beneath his feet; all flesh dissolved in spirit. Mary Magdalene, her arms wide, flings herself after him in a frenzy, longing to touch, to smell, to embrace in order to believe. She is a woman. She does not believe in the spirit. But he, the pure Spirit, turns from her and exclaims with a slight shudder: "*Noli me tangere!*" Is he afraid a woman's touch might bring his still wavering spirit back down to the level of the flesh?

A rocket cast a vivid light over the boat of flowers. I turned around; the recumbent women and the crouching men were momentarily lit with harsh violence and then immediately swallowed up by a still deeper darkness.

I examined the proffered women one by one. All had only one face—painted, daubed, decorated according to age-old traditions. Here the individual's masks are broken, the women lose their names, their ages, their ephemeral features; they have all dissolved into a hieratic synthesis, mysterious and eternal, into a sacred Kwannon heavily robed, with crude talismans and a motionless heart.

At Knossos, in Crete, a primitive statuette of a steatopygous woman has been found, a piece of magnetic iron thrust into the wound of her sex. On this boat of flowers, one feels everywhere that miraculous talisman, that magnetic iron, the motionless spiral that attracts. . . .

Around this mystical center cling the humble body, soul and mind; then come the tattoos, the jewels and the clothes; still later, the great peacock feather: love.

The boat again assumes the aspect of a prehistoric temple, a cavern at the water's edge, a moving altar consecrated to the lunar cult of the goddess who bears, tiered on her breast, the series of heavy breasts, pink as any sow's.

I no longer attempted to choose; I had understood. I crouched beside a woman, the first my foot had made contact with, and stretched out my hand. . . .

And immediately the woman stirred, half sat up as if she had suddenly been wrested from her torpor, threw back her pale head and began to sing. I saw her by the moon's greenish light, her head raised like a viper's.

She sang in a strange, strident voice—the lament of a wounded animal, the sad and passionate plaint of a bitch in heat, the inconsolable, the wild voice of the widow-woman left alone in the cave. Older than the heart or the mind, the entrails surrender to this appeal, which revives an age-old hunger no flesh can appease, recalling cave fires, stone axes. A wild beast leaps up in our loins, our totem: the jackal, the tiger or the wild boar.

Circe must have sung like that Chinese prostitute caterwauling as she stared at the water. She alone has been able to find the secret path back to the cave. Had Ulysses been a little more or less than what he was, he would never have returned.

"Joshiro! Joshiro!" I murmured, seized suddenly by an inexplicable desire. I lowered my eyelids and the vision of the young woman assailed me, ugly and cruel and so tempting! "Joshiro! Joshiro," I murmured, "why have you fallen so low?"

Again I heard her raucous, frenzied voice, amorously mingled with the clatter of swords. I was choking; I opened my eyes again, I saw the unknown woman staring at me impassively out of her white mask. Joshiro vanished. . . . Now I felt my feverish hand caressing that hard mask of the surrendering woman, that ardent, firm breast, those frail yet powerful knees.

The aversion that separates the races vanished. Suddenly I realized the impassable gulf could be bridged. I stood up and leaned on the railing with its lacquered panels; I too began to stare over the satiated woman's head at the lapping water.

It was not a woman I had caressed, it was Woman. She had been able to strip love of all its lying ornaments, all the cosmetics of a sickly sentimentality. No more angel's wings or arrows or roses: muscular, mud-spattered legs and a bestial, cruel face.

Pleasure, I discovered that evening, is not what the golden legend of the white race claims—a corporeal joy, the mutual fulfillment of the two sexes, camaraderie and the rest of such nonsense. Pleasure is a praying mantis, a pitiless struggle, an irreducible hatred of the two sexes, the two warring cosmic forces—the one that rises, the one that descends—engendering the Universe.

The man who seeks to raise his head toward heaven and the woman who embraces him, hissing, caterwauling like that Chinese woman, brings him down to earth.

The Japanese geishas attend a man in their lovemaking as if he were sick and they were about to cure him, or as if he were their son and they were giving him their breast to suck. The Chinese woman attends a man as if he were her mortal enemy, as if she had captured him in war and knew that there was no pity.

Circe must have been yellow and Chinese. How ingenuous and uninstructed the white sirens seem, how illiterate in their erotic lore, how unskillful and superficial, confusing love with sport or with the thirst for gold or happiness. Here voluptuousness exceeds all such minor pleasures; it exceeds the articulate word and returns to the savage cry, it sinks lower still to the great Roots, to the animal, the plants and to death.

> *The mouth of the serpent in the green bamboo,*
> *The sting of the yellow hornet—*
> *Faint is the evil that they can work;*
> *Much more venomous is the breast of woman . . .*

sings one old Chinese mouth.

"No, the breast of woman is not venomous," I thought in the warm and malodorous darkness of that flowing hair, that sweating body. "It is only the faithful, skillful servant of one of the two great forces it would be vain and sacrilegious to resist—of the force that draws us toward the earth.

"Blessed be this force! Blessed be the opposing force, too, which draws us upward out of our bodies! From their combat and their love is born that fantastic and beloved spectacle: the world."

Toward midnight I left the boat of flowers and I saw the stars again.

19

I CONTINUED my journey northward. I felt a little
sad and weary, but my heart was satisfied. Something in me was ripening in these painful yet commonplace
experiences.

I have always tried to let daily life penetrate me with the
impetuosity of extraordinary events. To contemplate the
stars, embrace a woman, drink a glass of cold water, eat a
slice of bread always gives me virgin sensations, the shock
of miracle.

I have always tried to see everything with eyes that are
constantly fresh. I was unconsciously following the com-
mandment of Ching Tang, so ineffably difficult in its simplicity; for this Chinese emperor had written this terrible
sentence on his bathtub: "Renew thyself every morning!"

I had rented a cart drawn by two oxen. My guide was a
calm old man with a scanty, drooping mustache and trousers
wrapped tight around his ankles. His name was Wang Lung.
I had chosen him because he had learned from his son, who

had returned from America, a few essential English words: I'm hungry, I'm thirsty, good, bad, yes, no, God, fire. We combined these words in a thousand different ways, we completed them with gestures and looks, and we nearly became friends. I had managed to make Wang Lung's black eyes human when they rested on me.

We had made our way across an enormous tranquil plain far from the river; an atmosphere of grave serenity, an invisible presence of eternal spirits had risen out of the earth. The dust in the sunshine, the stars in the night's coolness alternated in a ceremonial rhythm. And my blood gradually grew accustomed to this harmony and enjoyed an ancient happiness that I thought was lost forever.

How far we were from the fevered coasts, plague-ridden by the white men! Time, here in this calm solitude, had resumed its majestic course and its plantlike breathing. It scarcely moved, like deep waters gently flowing toward the sea. Time here had the gait of eternity; and everything that was steeped in its precious and stagnant substance became almost eternal. Here was the august face of the earth before the undesirable apparition of that buzzing and troublesome insect, man.

I pondered an Oriental legend as our cartwheels sank into the dust and gradually advanced. I remembered how one day, in India, night surprised me in a very poor village. The old men came and sat around me; a young man with gazelle's eyes knew English and served as our interpreter.

"Why do you travel?" one old man in a white turban asked me.

"To see the world."

"But you can see it at home."

"But I want all the world."

Then the old man began speaking to me with friendly irony: "Why all the world? Isn't the center of the earth, your country, enough for you? Travel through your own country and you'll travel around the world. Allow me to tell you an old story:

"The Mother of the Universe had two sons: the God of Wisdom and the God of War. Both wanted to sit on her knees.

" 'I cannot take you both,' the mother said. 'Go travel around the Universe; the one who comes back first will sit upon my knees.'

"The God of War leaped upon his charger and set off like an arrow. The God of Wisdom crouched at his mother's feet, heard his brother ride off at a gallop, stood up, bowed before his mother, circled about her three times and sat upon her knees.

"Years later, when the God of War returned, breathless and exhausted, and saw his brother upon his mother's knees, he flew into a rage.

" 'Why do you let him sit upon your knees?' he exclaimed. 'He's never left home!'

"And the mother answered: 'What counts, my son, is not to travel around the Universe, but around the center of the Universe!' "

The Chinese has followed this path of the God of Wisdom. Every morning he stands up, bows before the earth, gravely circles around her, and sits at evening upon her knees. His feet, his hands, his mind—like roots—are covered with earth. He sees, breathes, and sows the earth, like a woman. He venerates her like a benevolent Mother whose breasts are swollen with milk.

It is not the earth which belongs to him, as it does to the rest of us frivolous, rootless beings swept about by the wind, carried off on the pommel of the war god's saddle; it is he who belongs to the earth. All his life he serves the earth and when he dies, he returns to its heart, like seed, like a grain of wheat; he folds his hands, he receives the rain and the sun and he acts, with a tenfold force, upon the living.

Death is a whirlwind of invisible powers which you must conciliate by sacrifice and prayer—otherwise, beware!

All the ancestors, like inestimable treasures, are buried in the earth and lead an omnipotent existence there. The

Chinese feels them rise out of the earth and share his bread and his tears—the tremendous race of corpses that rules the living. The tomb is the fixed center around which life revolves.

"Man has the earth for his model!" Lao-tse exclaims. In winter, he falls with it into torpor; he is reborn with it in the spring; in the summer's orchard he ripens like a yellow melon.

The cold comes, the earth hardens, the trees are bare, the birds fly away or hide. The Chinese follows the great rhythm, he locks himself in his house, rests, waits. When it rains, he feels the rain penetrate his flesh and bones, steeping him like the earth.

"Guard the bridges! Close the road! Do not reveal that which is covered! Do not open the houses! Let everything be closed and locked!"

Thus in winter his ideas shrink, his morality grows stricter, actions permitted in spring are forbidden in wintertime. Everything contracts, becomes selfish, paltry, hard.

In spring, the earth blossoms, houses open, birds return, trees turn green again. The old poet is right: "No one can observe the five Buddhist commandments when the cherry trees are in bloom." Love caresses the body, morality broadens. The springtime festivals begin. In the old times, young men and girls picked orchids and flung themselves into the dance—a ritual, erotic dance accompanied by jousts and love songs.

> *For death, for life, for labor*
> *With you I unite*
> *I take your hands in mine*
> *With you I would grow old!*

In spring men forgot life's harshness and its bitter necessities; an intoxication rising out of the ground swelled all hearts. Men confronted life with generosity and courage:

> *Why say you have no cloak, my love?*
> *With you I share my own!*

We are crossing the interminable plain of the Yangtse, my guide and I, in silence. Life has kept only its most elementary functions and my heart adapts itself to them gratefully, as if it were returning, after so many detours, to the maternal house.

One evening I felt tired; the air was cool.

"Wang Lung," I exclaimed, "make a fire! I'm hungry!"

Wang Lung bowed his head, the cart stopped. We lit a fire; I sat down, legs crossed, and stared into the flames. The hyena's sinister laugh echoed in the distance, a jackal slipped through the underbrush.

Wang Lung lit his pipe and closed his eyes, facing the west. His thin, wrinkled face gleamed in the reflection of the flames.

"He's saying his prayers," I thought. "He's speaking to his God. He has mounted to the peak of his existence; he must not be disturbed!"

I forgot my hunger, I was ashamed of being inferior to this old man. He too must have been hungry, but he was mastering himself.

For a moment Wang Lung, disturbed by my silence, opened his eyes and stared at me.

"God?" I asked him, smiling.

"God!" he answered and closed his eyes again.

Then I took out my own praying stool, my notebook. I stared into the flames and wrote down all I had seen and felt during these last days. The two journeys: the visible one across China and the invisible one. . . .

Once I saw a Byzantine icon of St. George. The blond-haired young hero on his white horse, lance raised, was hurling himself against the dragon. All the bodies—St. George, the horse, the dragon—were compact, muscular, intense. A real drama, a bloody battle.

In the air above this real St. George was another St. George on another white horse, with another lance, facing another dragon. But in this upper level of vision, everything was dematerialized, the bodies were transparent and through them you saw the blossoming fields and the pale blue mountains in the distance.

This was a St. George more real than that of reality, the astral body of the action, the pale and immortal flower of matter.

I sensed, that evening as I sat in solitude before the flames, that double journey of my being. I saw, I touched the visible journey, all its details firmly fixed by matter. But the inner journey flickered half invisible, stripped of any solid body. I would have to catch it in words if it was not to be dispersed.

To mobilize those intrepid soldiers, the twenty-six letters of the alphabet, to besiege the breath, channel it, no longer to let it wander in the air. . . . Yes, I know, the finest essence cannot be caught in the net of words, but something still remains—a subtle perfume which stirs our senses and reveals the invisible.

I felt my heart broadened these last days by my contact with the earth in solitude. Something within me had ripened; someone within me had taken a step forward.

Leaning over my notebook, I tried to follow this line that had moved.

20

MANKIND

It is not you talking. Nor is it your race only which shouts within you, for all the innumerable races of mankind shout and rush within you: white, yellow, black.

Free yourself from race also; fight to live through the whole struggle of man. See how he has detached himself from the animal, how he struggles to stand upright, to coordinate his inarticulate cries, to feed the flame between his hearthstones, to feed his mind amid the bones of his skull.

Let pity overwhelm you for this creature who one morning detached himself from the ape, naked, defenseless, without teeth or horns, with only a spark of fire in his soft skull.

He does not know from where he comes or where he goes. But by loving, toiling, and killing, he wants to conquer the earth.

Look upon men and pity them. Look at yourself amid all men and pity yourself. In the obscure dusk of life we touch and fumble at each other, we ask questions, we listen, we shout for help.

We run. We know that we are running to die, but we cannot stop. We run.

We carry a torch and run. Our faces light up for a moment, but hurriedly we surrender the torch to our son, and then suddenly vanish and descend into Hades.

The mother looks ahead, toward her daughter; the daughter in turn looks ahead, beyond the body of her husband, toward her son—this is how the Invisible proceeds on earth.

We all look directly before us, ruthlessly, driven by dark, enormous, infallible powers behind us.

Rise above the improvised bastion of your body, look at the centuries behind you. What do you see? Hairy, blood-splattered beasts rising in tumult out of the mud. Hairy, blood-splattered beasts descending in tumult from the mountain summits.

The two bellowing armies meet like a man and a woman and become a lump of mud, blood, and brain.

Behold: multitudes ascend like grass out of the soil and fall into the soil again, fertile manure for future offspring. And the earth grows fat from the ashes, the blood, and the brains of man.

Numbers without end vanish in mid-journey; they are born, but they die barren. Huge pits suddenly gape in the darkness, multitudes tumble and fall, disorderly commands are heard in confused clamor, and the human herd stampedes and scatters.

Below and about us and within the abyss of our hearts we suddenly become aware of blind, heartless, brainless, ravenous powers.

We sail on a storm-tossed sea, and in a yellow lightning flash we feel we've entrusted our wealth, our children, and our gods to an eggshell.

The centuries are thick, dark waves that rise and fall, steeped in blood. Every moment is a gaping abyss.

*Gaze on the dark sea without staggering, confront
the abyss every moment without illusion or impudence or
fear.*

Without illusion, impudence, or fear. But this is not
enough; take a further step: battle to give meaning to the
confused struggles of man.

Train your heart to govern as spacious an arena as
it can. Encompass through one century, then through two
centuries, through three, through ten, through as many centuries as you can bear, the onward march of mankind. Train
your eye to gaze on people moving in great stretches of time.

Immerse yourself in this vision with patience, with
love and high disinterestedness, until slowly the world begins
to breathe within you, the embattled begin to be enlightened,
to unite in your heart and to acknowledge themselves as
brothers.

The heart unites whatever the mind separates,
pushes on beyond the arena of necessity and transmutes the
struggle into love.

Walk tiptoe on the edge of the insatiable precipice
and struggle to give order to your vision. Raise the multicolored trap door of the mystery—the stars, the sea, men and
ideas; give form and meaning to the formless, the mindless
infinitude.

Gather together in your heart all terrors, recompose
all details. Salvation is a circle; close it!

What is meant by happiness? To live every unhappiness. What is meant by light? To gaze with undimmed eyes
on all darknesses.

We are a humble letter, a single syllable, one word
out of a gigantic Odyssey. We are immersed in an enormous
song and we shine like humble pebbles as long as they remain immersed in the sea.

What is our duty? To raise our heads from the text
a moment, as long as our lungs can bear it, and to breathe
in the transoceanic song.

*To bring together all our adventures, to give mean-
ing to our voyage, to battle undauntedly with men, with gods,
with animals, and then slowly, patiently, to erect in our
brains, marrow of our marrow, our Ithaca.*

*Out of an ocean of nothingness, with fearful
struggle, the work of man rises slowly like a small island.*

*Within this arena, which grows more stable night
after day, generations work and love and hope and vanish.
New generations tread on the corpses of their fathers, continue the work above the abyss and struggle to tame the
dread mystery. How? By cultivating a single field, by kissing
a woman, by studying a stone, an animal, an idea.*

*Earthquakes come, the island sways, a corner crum-
bles away, another rises out of the sunless waves.*

*The mind is a seafaring laborer whose work is to
build a seawall in chaos.*

*From all these generations, from all these joys and
sorrows, from this lovemaking, these battles, these ideas, a
single voice rings out, pure and serene. Pure and serene
because, though it contains all the sins and disquietudes of
struggling man, it yet flies beyond them all and mounts
higher still.*

*Amidst all this human material Someone clambers
up on his hands and knees, drowned in tears and blood,
struggling to save himself.*

*To save himself from whom? From the body which
entwines him, from the people who support him, from the
flesh, from the heart and the brains of man.*

*"Lord, who are you? You loom before me like a
Centaur, his hands stretched toward the sky, his feet trans-
fixed in mud."*

"I am He who eternally ascends."

*"Why do you ascend? You strain every muscle, you
struggle and fight to emerge from the beast. From the beast,
and from man. Do not leave me!"*

*"I fight and ascend that I may not drown. I stretch
out my hands, I clutch at every warm body, I raise my head*

above my brains that I may breathe. I drown everywhere and can nowhere be contained."

"Lord, why do you tremble?"

"I am afraid! This dark ascent has no ending. My head is a flame that tries eternally to detach itself, but the breath of night blows eternally to put me out. My struggle is endangered every moment. My struggle is endangered in every body. I walk and stumble in the flesh like a traveler overtaken by night, and I call out: 'Help me!' "

THE EARTH

It is not you who call. It is not your voice calling from within your ephemeral breast. It is not only the white, yellow, and black generations of man calling in your heart. The entire Earth, with her trees and her waters, with her animals, with her men and her gods, calls from within your breast.

Earth rises up in your brains and sees her entire body for the first time.

She shudders; she is a beast that eats, begets, moves, remembers. She hungers, she devours her children—plants, animals, men, thoughts—she grinds them in her dark jaws, passes them through her body once more, then casts them again into the soil.

She recalls her passions and broods upon them. Her memory unfolds within my heart; it spreads everywhere and conquers time.

It is not the heart which leaps and throbs in the blood. It is the entire Earth. She turns her gaze backward and relives her dread ascent through chaos.

I recall an endless desert of infinite and flaming matter. I am burning! I pass through immeasurable, unorganized time, completely alone, despairing, crying in the wilderness.

And slowly the flame subsides, the womb of matter grows cool, the stone comes alive, breaks open, and a small green leaf uncurls into the air, trembling. It clutches the soil, steadies itself, raises its head and hands, grasps the air, the water, the light, and sucks at the Universe.

It sucks at the Universe and wants to pass it through its body—thin as a thread—to turn it into flower, fruit, seed. To make it deathless.

The sea shudders and is torn in two; out of its muddy depths a voracious, restless, and eyeless worm ascends.

The weight of matter is conquered, the slab of death heaves high, and armies of trees and beasts emerge filled with lust and hunger.

I gaze upon Earth with her muddy brain, and I shudder as I relive the peril. I might have sunk and vanished amid these roots that suck at the mud blissfully; I might have smothered in this tough and many-wrinkled hide; or I might have twitched eternally within the bloody, dark skull of the primordial ancestor.

But I was saved. I passed beyond the thick-leaved plants, I passed beyond the fishes, the birds, the beasts, the apes. I created man.

I created man, and now I struggle to be rid of him.

"I am cramped and crushed! I want to escape!" This cry destroys and fructifies the bowels of the earth eternally. It leaps from body to body, from generation to generation, from species to species, becoming always stronger and more carnivorous. All parents shout: "I want to give birth to a son greater than I!"

During those fearful moments when the Cry passes through our bodies, we feel a prehuman power driving us ruthlessly. Behind us a muddy torrent roars, full of blood, tears, and sweat, filled with squeals of joy, of lust, of death.

An erotic wind blows over Earth, a giddiness overpowers all living creatures till they unite in the sea, in caves, in the air, under the ground, transferring from body to body a great, incomprehensible message.

Only now, as we feel the onslaught behind us, do we begin dimly to apprehend why the animals fought, begot, and died; and behind them the plants; and behind these the huge reserve of inorganic forces.

We are moved by pity, gratitude, and esteem for our old comrades-in-arms. They toiled, loved, and died to open a road for our coming.

We also toil with the same delight, agony, and exaltation for the sake of Someone Else who with every courageous deed of ours proceeds one step farther.

All our struggle once more will have a purpose much greater than we, wherein our toils, our miseries, and our crimes will have become useful and holy.

This is an onslaught! A Spirit rushes, storms through matter and fructifies it, passes beyond the animals, creates man, digs its claws into his head like a vulture, and shrieks.

It is our turn now. It molds us, pummels matter within us and turns it into spirit, tramples on our brains, mounts astride our sperm, kicks our bodies behind it, and struggles to escape.

It is as though the whole of life were the visible, eternal pursuit of an invisible Bridegroom who from body to body hunts down his untamed Bride, Eternity.

And we, all the guests of the wedding procession—plants, animals, men—rush trembling toward the mystical nuptial chamber. We each carry with awe the sacred symbols of marriage—one the Phallos, another the Womb.

21

I HAVE GROWN DRUNK on an exotic wine—made of dates, bananas, rice and a few drops of heavy and mysterious blood.

Was it the real Peking that I reached so laboriously and at such lengths? Or was that Peking only the blue smoke of my intoxication?

I left Wang Lung and his cart for I was suddenly impatient; a foreboding made my body feverish.

The spring was tender as a young bamboo shoot; the wisteria hung in scented clusters above the garbage heaps; flowering acacia besieged the crumbling old walls; and out of the depth of the purple sky flew flocks of crows that had smelled the great carrion from far away.

The evening star palpitated like a heart. On the lintel of the city's great gate were painted the three ritual ideograms, so absurd in this poverty: *Tai Ha Men,* the Great Gate of Happiness. Their black lines interlaced and stiffened over my head like a nest of serpents.

Filthy and bearded Tibetans, giant Manchus, sullen and taciturn Mongols, slender and shameless Chinese; Buddhist priests in their earth-colored robes; men and women of the desert, their skinny, nervous legs, their long eyes brimming with solitude.

Asses, goats, hogs, buffaloes wallowing in the mud. Fermented urine, rancid castor oil and the acrid exhalation of human sweat. The smell of China. The wind blows and the walls, the temples, the tombs crumble, and the dust of the dead catches in your throat.

I surrender to this river of tiny, slanting eyes, of smells, and of colors. . . .

"Patience . . . patience . . ." I told myself. "Don't hold your nose; breathe. Tao, the divine essence, penetrates and purifies all ordure. Don't forget what the wise Confucius replied to his disciple:

"But where is what you call the Tao found?"

"There is nothing on earth, in heaven and in hell where the Tao is not found."

"But tell me exactly where."

"Well, for instance, it's in this little ant. And lower still!"

"In this blade of grass?"

"Lower still!"

"In this pebble?"

"Lower still!"

"Well then, in human excrement!"

The smell of China persists, clinging to my nostrils; its divine origin does not console me. But ultimately one must resign oneself to it. The entire rind of this marvelous earth is composed of human excrement. It too, it above all, is made divine in this universal embrace of the Tao.

Religious books speak of it with insistence and respect. Chou-Li, the sacred book, minutely prescribed three thousand years ago the rites concerning the elaboration and use of human excrement—"the basis of Chinese civilization."

Often, when passing through Chinese villages, I have thought of those sacred pages in order to be able to endure the unendurable. For thousands of years China has religiously observed the law of this circular movement, and she has flourished. Nothing is wasted; everything turns and returns, in different forms, immortal. Life is a cistern in which the single element, the Tao, in infinite combinations, creates, destroys and re-creates flowers, ordure and the gods.

All is one; happy the man who under the countless and flowing masks can discern this immutable unity. Then he will bow, with respect, to human excrement.

In despair that evening, I took refuge in these thoughts in order to distract my attention from my senses; I did not completely succeed and looked about with impatience to find a path through this crowd.

Suddenly my friend Li-Te, riding in his ricksha, dashed forward to help me. He shook my hand and greeted me in a cordial, dry tone. As always, he spoke very little, remaining polite and distant. But in his tiny black eyes there was something new which disturbed me: a new touch of steel.

"I shouldn't have accepted his invitation," I told myself, as I expressed aloud my delight at seeing him again; it transformed me, I assured him, back into the young student at Oxford.

He smiled; his white teeth flashed for a second.

"Yes," he said. "Oxford, our youth . . . the blond girls, the beer . . ." And he pressed his lips tight.

An old coolie bowed before me; I climbed into his ricksha.

The acacias perfumed the evening air. Peking hummed like a hive disgorging its furious bees. Flamboyant posters writhed over our heads—long red-and-black banners with huge interlacing characters, sinister and attractive, as if this strange alphabet were some shadowy jungle in which embraced or fought the age-old serpents of knowledge.

We hurried through the crowded streets, Li-Te ahead. My eyes were fascinated by my coolie's back, which swayed to the right and left as heavy drops of sweat ran down his tattered body. I cocked my ears, and above the murmur of

Peking I heard his broad soles clattering across disjointed tiles or splashing through the mud.

Li-Te noticed my eyes fixed on my coolie's ravaged back. "They're our beasts of burden," he said, his teeth flashing again. "And yours, too . . ." he added after a brief hesitation.

The sinister smile flickered across his delicate and carefully etched lips.

I didn't answer, but I was ashamed. Suddenly I felt that both were degraded: the man who pulls, the man who lets himself be pulled.

To comfort myself a little I quickly found an excuse. "As long as the world exists," I told my friend, "I'm afraid there will be coolies in one form or another. White men, too, have their beasts of burden with human faces. Such injustice is inherent in social life. But rebellion, too, praise God! comes out against such injustice. Afterwards comes the new injustice, in another class, under another mask. It is only the changing of the mask which we triumphantly, and how briefly, call emancipation and freedom."

Li-Te suddenly turned around and looked at me. That new thing, that touch of steel gleamed and immediately vanished in his eyes. Some hidden mechanism grated in his flesh but he quickly controlled himself.

"Yes," he murmured and said no more.

Immediately I remembered one evening in a little students' restaurant in Oxford. Joshiro, whom Li-Te had desired for some time, was dancing shamelessly before him, in the arms of a handsome young Englishman. Li-Te watched her a long while, and the muscles of his face remained motionless.

But suddenly he took a penknife out of his pocket, bent over, and under the table thrust it three times slowly into his thigh.

But now there was something new in him. Li-Te no longer took out a knife; he no longer recovered his equilibrium by shedding his seething blood. He repressed, he digested, he no longer wasted a drop of his strength; he collected himself, preparing to spring.

I had seen, crudely painted on the walls of a cave in Africa, a lion on the prowl. He raised one of his front paws, coiling it like a spring ready to unfurl. His yellow eyes, seemingly somnolent, brooded on an invisible prey.

"I shouldn't have accepted his invitation," I told myself again. "He is no longer my friend. A new demon possesses him. I see the lion's paw in his eyes."

22

A PRINCELY GATE, freshly painted red, wide open. The little streets around it are choked with a crowd in fantastic rags. Mendicant monks, leaning on their long, belled staffs, hold out empty bowls, chanting under their breath. Naked children, boys and girls, wallow in a puddle at the crossroads along with pale piglets and blue-green ducks. Long rows of rickshas are to the right and left of the gate, the crouching coolies smoking, benumbed by their dreams.

"My father's house!" Li-Te announced, leaping out of his ricksha.

And as I stared in surprise at this festive décor, my friend reassured me: "No, it's not in your honor!" he whispered, and I thought I detected a note of irony in his voice. "Today my father is celebrating his eightieth birthday. You have come at a propitious time. Kindly cross our threshold, my friend!"

A confused babble, muffled drumbeats, shrill flutes, droning voices. From top to bottom, the entire courtyard was gaily decorated with long gold-lettered banners.

Li-Te began translating them for me with a slightly weary expression: " 'May the great gods of light long preserve you on the earth!' 'Sons, grandsons and great-grandsons . . .' 'You are the blessed tree covered with flowers and fruit.'

"These are the silk banners my father's friends have sent him, along with pigeons, cakes and rare manuscripts. But please, come and greet the old one!"

I bowed before the old mandarin. He was sitting enthroned in a deep armchair delicately carved with dragons. He was enormously fat with a scanty beard and drooping mustache, his hands marvelously beautiful. He looked like an old, very sad Buddha.

The great hall was crowded: gentlemen in silk robes, elegant ladies; a strong odor of jasmine and musk. A gathering of many-colored exotic birds.

At the rear, on an improvised stage, a troupe of young actors performed an old comedy: handsome, painted boys played the *femmes fatales*, ferocious bandits, perverse and hypocritical monks; their voices were hideously nasal. The shrill flutes accompanied every one, unconcerned with these all too human passions.

The old mandarin smiled and spoke a few words in Chinese.

"He is pleased," Li-Te explained. "He begs you to excuse his ignorance of foreign languages. He says he can only smile at you."

Servants circulated among the guests and offered tiny cups of jasmine tea on lacquered trays. People laughed, whispered, smoked or nibbled roasted melon seeds.

I glanced unobserved at my friend Li-Te. His masklike expression was more emphatic, his eyes darker. His gaze was always remote, motionless, fixed.

He must work hard, I thought; he must be obsessed by a great effort. Is he fighting the Reds? Is he fighting his rascally and powerful brothers, the Japanese?

"Dear friend," I said, "the Japanese actors made a deep

127

impression on me, but I could not understand why their voices were so artificially nasal. Now I see: they were imitating you."

Li-Te growled between his teeth. "Monkeys . . ."

"Li-Te," I said to sound out my friend, "Li-Te, why this implacable hatred of Japan?"

"It is not hatred," Li-Te murmured, "it is contempt."

"They are your brothers."

"Are you a pacifist?"

"War is a terrible thing; I have seen it!"

"Yes, terrible," Li-Te replied, "but effective. It accelerates the course of things, it mobilizes the great virtues, it can transform the wretched little bourgeois into a hero. Besides . . ."

"Besides?"

"It's here; it's the only reality. The warrior, the man resolved to deal and suffer death. The others are nothing but misfits. Let them rot."

"Joshiro . . ." I began.

At this Li-Te suddenly wheeled, his face rigid. "I know," he said; "she's back."

"Joshiro loves China and works for her liberation. Couldn't you two reach some understanding? I'm supposed to meet her here in China," I added, purposely distorting Joshiro's words a little.

"Where?" Li-Te said with a sudden excitement he could not control.

"Here in Peking."

"In Peking!" Li-Te exclaimed, and I could hear the anger in his voice.

He said no more, and a sardonic smile soon parted his lips. "We'll see . . ." he growled. "We'll see."

I could not understand. I found this anger excessive. Could it be love so dreadfully disguised as hate? And how did this strong man, who felt so deeply his responsibility to his threatened country, deign to consider his own emotional problems?

"Li-Te," I said, determined to plumb this mystery, but at that moment my friend stood up.

"My uncle Kung Ta-hen," he said.

Half a century ago, this old mandarin was attached to the Chinese Embassy in Paris. He spoke an amazingly old-fashioned French. He began to chat as he sat down between Li-Te and me, his tiny affable eyes twinkling.

"The Communists," I said to him in a low voice, to stir him out of his somnolent beatitude, "are advancing in China. Tonight's dispatches are alarming. A great province has fallen into their hands."

The old man smiled.

"Russia is ephemeral," he said; "China is eternal."

"Japan," I added in a dismayed voice, "covets the Chinese coastline and will have it. Japan is a terrible enemy!"

"Japan is ephemeral; China is eternal."

"But a few years ago the Yangtse overflowed—thirty million perished."

"Yes, yes. But China is eternal."

A girl approached us, mincing gracefully on her tiny mutilated feet in their embroidered slippers. She looked like a wounded bird. She was wearing a honey-yellow silk gown and her heavy hair had blue glints in it. Her smile mingled an ineffable melancholy with its sweetness. She bowed.

"My sister Siu-lan," my friend said. "You can talk to her; she understands a little English."

A strange emotion welled up in me. I felt the astral body of this girl voluptuously penetrate the invisible and palpitating envelope of my own body.

Where had I seen her? Nowhere. But her fluid, tremulous face was a marvelous contrast to the fixed countenance I seek here on earth.

The mystery of that ardor to unite that which we call love has always seemed to me a kind of terrible reminiscence; an order given by some cave ancestor; a Jew wandering through centuries and bodies, desperately seeking. One of my ancestors must have loved and been unable to possess a woman who resembled this Chinese girl quivering before me.

"Siu-lan," I murmured to myself, and my flesh was satisfied.

Like the sorceresses of the old imperial courts in China, who, from the odor of the newcomers, discovered whether they were friends or enemies, my soul sensed in Siu-lan a gentle, infinitely ancient perfume that I thought had evaporated from the world forever; a body that would adapt profoundly to the curves and hollows of my own.

I have always hated romantic feathers that make this insatiable monster ridiculous, for it is neither beautiful nor gentle nor pure.

"Oh my master!" I exclaimed. "You annihilate all things without cruelty; you give abundantly without kindness! You are older than the remotest antiquity and you are not old. You fashion all shapes without skill!

"It is you we call Love!"

Siu-lan offered me a cup of tea. With sudden ardor I took the cup in both hands. At that moment a boy leaped onto the stage. He was very handsome, heavily made up, with long perverse eyes. He looked like the young Buddhas I had seen in the gloom of Hindu temples: hermaphroditic, with a woman's disturbing breasts, a voluptuous, ambiguous smile.

He began to perform a shameless dance; never could words or music express with such frenzy the power of desire and the intoxicating joy of living.

I turned toward Siu-lan with a questioning look. She lowered her eyes, confused.

"That is the demon!" she murmured a few seconds later. "The Tempter, Spirit of Evil."

"I thought it was love," I said, smiling. "He resembles him so!"

"No, no! It is the Demon, the Spirit of Evil!" she insisted.

"While love is the Spirit of Good, is that it?"

Siu-lan smiled. "I don't know," she said.

A servant girl came up, out of breath: "Siu-lan, your father is calling you!" she exclaimed.

I turned and saw the old mandarin watching us, nervously fluttering his fan. He had suddenly become sadder and older.

I smiled at him and bowed; but his motionless eyes only stared, troubled and enormous.

23

$\mathcal{A}$ LITTLE SITTING ROOM overlooking the garden.
The windows are open, the sun already shining
into the courtyard. Two canaries begin singing as the light
touches their gilded cage. The old gardener comes and goes,
lingering over each bush. Tenderly he straightens it, removes
a tiny dry branch; he caresses it. His eye is sure and full of
love.

Siu-lan, Li-Te and I sip our aromatic tea in delicate old
cups. At the bottom of the cup appears a menacing yellow
dragon.

Old paintings on silk glow where they hang on the wall. I
cannot make them out clearly in the blue morning shadows,
but at the rear in a niche I joyfully recognize a statuette of
Kwannon, goddess of mercy.

Siu-lan poured me more tea. Then she sat down and
leaned toward me.

I started—how much Siu-lan resembled Kwannon! Her
oval face, her slanting eyes, her sensual lips, her brows bran-

dished like sharp swords—the same austerity mingled with gentleness, the same aristocratic and welcoming expression.

"Kwannon . . . Kwannon," I murmured, shuddering.

My heart could never have created such a goddess of mercy—sure, disdainful, motionless. She does not cure pain by acting; she does not bring the miserable consolation. This Kwannon is a goddess who cures the human heart, sitting motionless on her throne. Merely seeing her is enough to make you forget all pain.

She tilted her head slightly, as if her large Buddha-like ears were listening to human suffering from some great distance, and Buddha's daughter smiles for she knows that suffering too is an illusion, like happiness—that you will awaken and that suffering will vanish like a dream. You will vanish too, and the Universe, and the Cause of the Universe.

I looked at Kwannon and I felt my heart overflowing in reply. I was happy. Time, in my breast, had stopped.

"She's Japanese," I said mechanically, indicating the lovely statuette.

"No," Siu-lan said, timid yet firm. "No, she's Chinese."

Li-Te was sitting opposite me, his face calm and inscrutable; I sensed his eyes fixed on me without tenderness.

Silence. The air was heavy, filled with unspoken questions. In the space between Li-Te and me I felt a new and invisible struggle.

Siu-lan was sitting between us. She wore a blue gown with wide embroidered sleeves and silver buttons. Her father, she told us, regretted that he could not join us for tea; he had had a bad dream and was feeling sorrowful.

Suddenly Li-Te raised his voice, while Siu-lan looked up at her brother with a pleading expression.

"What new sensation are you seeking in China? For I know you, old friend. You're a pirate, and you rove the seas like a true white man."

I said nothing. How could I make this determined and practical yellow man understand the vague, profound anxieties of my being? I sensed his attachment to a positive goal;

133

he was surely one of the leaders of the Kuomintang. He had a specific purpose: to liberate his country from the White Men or the Yellow; to waken his people; to make them worthy of freedom and justice. Every day he took a step toward this goal. He saw, he touched, he could measure the progress of his mind. The upper invisible story was missing. His soul had only a ground floor, so how could he understand me?

Li-Te lit a cigarette, raised it to his mouth two or three times, and nervously stubbed it out in the ashtray.

"The best opium?" he sneered. "Are you looking for the best opium here? Oblivion? Yellow poison?"

(Yes, yes, the yellow poison. . . . Inject that powerful virus into my bloodstream. . . . Annex China to my soul. . . . Take the cure.)

"No!" I answered.

"That's good! You would be disappointed. We are no longer exotics. We yellow men suffer too—from the white poison. Cannons, hunger, anger . . . the itch of justice and of liberty . . ."

"I am an apolitical animal."

"What do you want, then? To see the beauties of China: palaces, temples, *bibelots*, porcelains, Buddha? Haven't you finished your beauty-hunt yet?"

(No doubt he wanted to add "Aren't you ashamed?" but had restrained himself.)

Li-Te fell silent. I looked at Siu-lan; she had lowered her eyes, embarrassed. Her delicate nostrils quivered. Her whole being anxiously awaited a reply.

"I have finished all my services," I answered. "I am a free man. I have no illusions. I hope for nothing. I abstain from the struggle, not out of unconcern or cowardice, but because I know."

"What is it that you know?"

"The end of all things."

Li-Te hissed like a snake. "In our age of steel—steel and petroleum and gas—you mustn't think too much. We are at the beginning of things. Let us leave the end—philosophy, metaphysics, the higher inaction—to the generations that will come at the end!

"We were born in an age of war; let us fight, then. Without intellectual shilly-shallying, let us take our battle positions. Let us choose; right or left matters little, but let us choose!"

(Yes, I knew all these watchwords. My ears have often rung with them, but behind them I saw perfidy and the void. And I have remained alone. Even among my friends, especially among my friends, I feel I am an undesirable. A hand reluctant to draw a salary; an eye that sees clearly.)

I turned toward Li-Te. "What is it that you have done, O man of action, during the ten long years we have not seen each other?"

Li-Te bit his lips. His eyes flickered; for a second I felt him lost in some terrible vision, the enormous cadaver of China . . . Empire, Republic, Communism? No, instead, some huge thing decomposing. The generals sell themselves—Japanese yen, English pounds, rubles, dollars—they stroll from one camp to the next, to the highest bidder, dragging behind them a long file of ragged coolies.

Li-Te shook his head; tiny drops of sweat beaded his forehead.

"Nothing!" he answered furiously. "Nothing! And you?"

I started. My life? Journeys, a blood-colored line across the continents. A heart seeking itself in space and losing its way, a soul unashamed to confess itself in print and to fling itself to the swine in tiny mouthfuls. A scribe! A life of white paper and black ink. A prostituted soul!

"Nothing . . ." I answered in a low voice.

Heavy silence. The two canaries had stopped singing. I could hear Siu-lan sigh faintly. She stood up in silence on the toes of her tiny feet, like a dancer. She laid two roses between Li-Te and me and poured tea into our empty cups. Then she sat down calmly; submissive and omnipotent, she had fulfilled her woman's duty.

The scent of the roses spread in the envenomed air. Sweetness, happiness; the woman brought an ineffable presence between the men attacking each other without respect or pity, the two roses her supreme argument.

For a moment I closed my eyes to let the irrefutable rose sink deeper within me and I continued the appeal I had begun yesterday upon seeing Siu-lan.

"O my master! You have an infinity of hands that attract and repel, that pray, promise and threaten, that caress, wound and caress again. . . . You come bringing two roses at the terrible and futile moment when men dispute. O my master! O my master, O love!"

I opened my eyes again. Li-Te had left the room; Siu-lan, a little wan, leaned on the window sill overlooking the garden and inhaled the earth with pent-up avidity.

At the other end of the garden, her old father was smoking in a blissful torpor; the tiny grains of opium hissed in the earthenware bowl. You could hear the pipe gurgling. The two gold canaries threw back their heads and began to sing, free, happy, one beside the other, competing for love.

24

"Siu-lan," I murmured.

She turned back to me and realized we were alone; for a second, a vague expression of fear ran across her face, but then she smiled.

"Are you frightened, Siu-lan?"

"No," she answered, blushing. "Why should I be frightened?" She lowered her head, confused. A quiver ran through her young body.

"Love," I told myself—"the great vulture. . . . Its powerful black and yellow wings extend, and the air trembles. . . ."

At that moment Siu-lan's favorite cat pushed open the door and noiselessly advanced, supple yet strong as a young lioness. Siu-lan started, then happily picked up the cat in her arms and sat down near the window, reassured. She was no longer frightened, she was no longer alone; the great wings she had just heard above her had folded again.

She looked into my eyes and her smile did not waver. "Japan . . . Tell me about Japan," she pleaded.

At the perfume of that breath, my memory blossomed; Japan rose up out of the waves with hallucinatory intensity. But as I still said nothing, Siu-lan insisted, her voice caressing:

"What was the greatest pleasure you had there in the 'country of the dwarfs?' What was your greatest sorrow? Please, tell me about it."

I don't remember what I said but I remember my hands and their enveloping gestures and the breathless ardor of my voice, and above all I remember the air that came between Siu-lan and me. Never have I felt a more plastic element under the palm of my hand as when that mass of blue air materialized, became a precious substance, like jade, took form and followed the curves, the sinuous aspirations of my thought!

Suddenly Japan appeared before me like a concrete and living organism, every vague detail dissolved into a solid whole; the multiform mass of my Japanese experience had assumed a face.

"Siu-lan," I said, "the vision of Japan has changed within me, it has been completed, enlarged, it has assumed a more human savor—I mean, one that is more intimate and bitter."

"Why?" Siu-lan murmured without raising her head.

"Perhaps because I myself have become more human and consequently more intimate and bitter!" I answered, with a smile to conceal my emotion.

The sad memories floated up from the depths of my eyes and my ears and my aching hands.

And among these associations one in particular, the saddest of all, caught at my heart.

I must have described this memory aloud, for gradually Siu-lan's eyes clouded and filled with tears.

"A man without children," a Japanese told me one day, "never knows the *Ah!* of things."

"Far away, Siu-lan, in another country, I was once crossing the snow-covered peaks of Mount Athos, the holy mountain with its austere Byzantine monasteries. Suddenly I found myself in front of a hermit's cave. Inside there was nothing but a huge iron cross, two holy idols and a pitcher of water. At the cave's mouth crouched the shivering old hermit. I stopped and we exchanged a few words.

" 'Your life is very hard, O holy anchorite,' I told him. 'You must suffer greatly.'

" 'I? Suffer?' the hermit answered, shaking his head. 'Do you call this suffering?' And he pointed to his frozen feet, his rags, and the nakedness of the cave. 'This is nothing, my son. These are trifles. Suffering is another thing.'

" 'What thing, my father?'

" 'To have a child and lose it. That is the only *Ah!* in the world.'

"But one evening in a dreadful neighborhood of Tokyo, I myself learned another *Ah!*, one deeper and heavier still, for it degrades and dishonors us all.

"Faces heavily painted with rice powder, thousands of unreal masks that emerge half strangled from the doors, calling plaintively, necks stretched, eyes swollen. . . .

"For weeks I was obsessed by the desire to see this wretched district where yellow flesh is sold. But I could not overcome my disgust. The diseases of the body and the soul, human degradation fills me with indignation. Not for those wretches who suffer, but toward the human nature that can fall so low, for the soul and the flesh without the strength to resist.

"But one evening I was ashamed of my weakness; I took my heart in my hands and leaped into a taxi:

" 'Tamanoi!' I cried to the driver.

"It was raining gently and night had fallen— a tragic night. In the various countries where I have fed my five senses the nights have a different savor.

"In India night is a tigress slinking out of the jungle and howling amorously as she prowls around the villages. And in the stupas, the great monasteries, the *biku* in his saffron robes chants the evening hymn, 'the melody of the tiger,' that is insinuating, monotonous and filled with dread.

"In Africa, night is an ogress, her enormous breasts rich

with black milk. And men, satiated, fall at her feet, their fists clenched.

"In Andalusia, I surprised the night fluttering above the flaming pomegranate trees, like a blue bird with a long, starry tail. And in Greece, the night is like a flowering lemon tree.

"But here, in Tamanoi, night is a hyena—something between a hyena and a woman weeping.

"Dim, winding alleyways, each narrower than the next, a nauseating stink of phenic acid and sweat. Thousands of worm-eaten huts are on every side and from the peephole of each door emerges a woman's head—a terrifying, spectral apparition smiling at the long files of men passing. Old men, young men, boys. . . .

"The smile is frozen, crusted in the rice powder and the coagulated lipstick. It does not move or change expression, it stays the same, rigid all night long. Sometimes the mouth manages to open; then you can hear the whole desiccated crust of the face cracking.

"I walk past rapidly. I cannot endure the horror. Pharmacies, beauty parlors, tobacco and sake shops. My feet splash through puddles. I had bought two big red apples to keep me company and give me courage; I clutch them, cool in my hands and sweet-smelling, and I feel a strange consolation.

"I force my eyes to look directly at these motionless, bluish heads in the humid air.

"At Yoshiwara, that higher-class bazaar of female flesh, the spectacle is not so terrible. The little wooden huts are clean; a barker sitting on his ankles in front of each door praises his merchandise and gives its price. 'One yen, one yen! Look at the photographs! The finest geisha. One yen, one yen! Look at the photographs! Choose for yourself!'

"I examine the photographs. In front of each door, a long coffin-shaped window. Behind the glass, lit by tiny colored bulbs, are enormous photographs of smiling geishas, and since they are leaning against the back of the window in mauve, blue or green light, they look like drowned women floating in the depths of the sea.

"Yes, the spectacle at Yoshiwara is pathetic, but from time to time you hear a little laughter or the notes of the *samisen*, like the dry squawks of birds of prey. And behind the screens of the walls, you sometimes hear a woman singing.

> *Okao ni usubeni tsuketa to sa*
> *sano, sano, tsuketa to sa . . .*
>
> *She has painted her face pink today,*
> *La-la-la, pink today . . .*

"But here at Tamanoi it is stifling. Here the women's mouths remain motionless, their eyes are wide and fixed. You approach, and in them discover a mute, animal suffering. . . .

"Siu-lan, that night at Tamanoi poisoned my heart. All those heads sticking out of all those doors seemed to be suffering the terrible torture of an iron yoke. Yes, all those women, our wretched sisters, were bearing the iron yoke of the city—all those hovels, Tamanoi, Tokyo, you and I, all humanity. . . .

"I felt covered with shame. Cowardly. We men had let women assume the whole responsibility. We had let them fight at the most dangerous posts; and we, like cowards, had taken cover behind them.

"Suddenly, in those dreadful alleyways, Buddha crept past like a long look.

"But it was not the Buddha we love; he was not shining in the flower of his youth, he did not have a sensual mouth or laughing eyes. He was old, sad, merciful as death.

"Then I was able to overcome my disgust. I walked toward a painted head and I stared straight into those eyes, forcing myself to smile. Was she young, old? Was she beautiful? Through that thick, frozen mask it was impossible to reach the face. But I saw that she had human eyes.

"Once in a distant northern city, I had seen an old baboon

behind the bars of a zoo. I would always find her crouching near the door, one hand on her cheek; she stared at me with enormous sadness. I was young then, and cruel, but thanks to that baboon I began to understand the pain you sometimes see in human eyes. Now and then she coughed; her breasts were two withered pouches. She stared at me and from her agonized being and her human eyes rose one terrifying and simple question: Why? Why?

"I shook my head to drive away that abominable vision. Again I saw the painted head before me and I managed to smile. The woman took heart. She said something. I had not understood what it was, but the intonation of her voice was so suppliant that I felt as if the wall between us had collapsed.

"And in truth, the tiny, worm-eaten door opened and, without realizing it, I found myself sitting on the old matting. I looked around me; I remembered the hermit's cave in the other holy Tamanoi, Mount Athos—here there were a few photographs of American sailors, a pitcher of water and a mattress.

"It was cold, the woman closed the peephole, knelt in silence, and pushed a tiny lit stove in front of me."

25

A sob. I started. Japan vanished and I found myself back in that peaceful garden in Peking on a sunny day. Siu-lan had buried her face in her lap and was crying.

I bent over her tenderly.

"Siu lan, Siu-lan, don't cry."

I was seized with an irresistible desire to touch that ivory neck beneath the delicately curved hair, to feel a woman's hot tears on my fingertips.

But just as I stretched my hand, I heard someone cough in the garden. I turned around and saw the old father, his neck extended, his lips slack, staring at us with his dead eyes, an indescribable terror spread over his whole face.

At that moment I understood the hideous martyrdom of the old mandarin. He, the fanatic conservative who doubtless every night raised his arms to heaven and prayed to his old ancestors—"O great powers of China, cast the White Devils into the sea!"—now saw the cursed race in his own house, at the side of his adored daughter.

"She is mine," I growled between my teeth. "She is more than your daughter, more than a Chinese girl; she is a woman. She is one of the two wings of the great universal power that engenders life; I am the other. We shall unite the pair, whether you like it or not."

Suddenly I stood up and tried to laugh.

"Siu-lan," I said, "I remind myself of those public story-tellers I see every evening in the streets of Peking. They tell their sad or funny story and act out all the characters. Like one-man bands. Depending on the mood of their tale, they weep, laugh, change before our startled eyes into princes, beggars, devils, girls. And the crowd's naïve tears flow in buckets. I have made you cry, Siu-lan. Forgive me. But if you like, I shall turn the page and tell you a funny story that will make you laugh. All right?"

"No!" she said abruptly. "No, I would rather cry."

A second later in a low voice: "How sad it is being a woman!"

"No, not always," I answered, smiling. "The very next day after that night of hell, I found one of the loveliest smiles that still exist on our sad planet—the smile of the geisha. I was strolling through the Asakusa neighborhood, in downtown Tokyo. The great temple of Kwannon was alive with noise, like the roar of a bull. Priests were beating drums, a swarming crowd clapped its hands, tossed coins into a huge wooden trough and prayed, hands pressed together.

"This little Kwannon, a black statuette, was taken from the sea by fishermen thirteen centuries ago. It had been set here under a humble roof, a fisherman's cottage, and has since become a colossal temple. Around this temple rise the eternal huts of man where food and drinks, toys and miraculous talismans are sold—everything man needs to resist death a little.

"I wandered slowly among this crowd, under enormous red lanterns. Two gigantic camphorwood demons at the temple gates stared at the crowd and grinned ferociously.

"The temple's wooden steps gleamed, polished smooth by

the contact of countless bare feet. I mingled with the murmuring faithful who squatted on their ankles and chanted under their breath the magic phrase: *Namu myo ho reghenkyo . . . Namu myo ho reghenkyo . . .*

" 'What does that chant mean?' I asked a sly-looking monk who had taken my arm on the temple steps.

" 'Glory to the Lotus of Truth!'

" 'But beyond that?'

" 'It is the watchword, do you understand? When you knock at the gate of paradise, and you hear within the terrible voice—*Who is there?*—you recite the password *Namu myo ho reghenkyo* and the gate will open.'

" 'Are you sure?'

"The cunning monk blinked his little eyes at me.

" 'Quite sure!' he answered, smiling, and waited to see if I would join him in his mockery.

"But I was watching these men and women kneeling on the temple matting under the lanterns. I stared at their ecstatic faces, gleaming with certainty and joy; these men and women were freed of their sordid interests, their petty joys and sorrows. They had already entered paradise. What need had these souls of a paradise after death? They had already entered paradise, the paradise of ecstasy's instantaneous immortality.

"I watched them and murmured between my teeth these words of some sage or other: 'If you believe you have found salvation, you have found it; if you believe you have not found it, you have not found it.'

"Yes, it was all beautiful as I came and went among this happy crowd, yet I felt sick at heart. Behind these gods and these lanterns I distinguished two motionless eyes watching me in anguish. I saw a painted mouth, an open wound that cried to me: *Help!* Tamanoi was there in the middle of the temple—Tamanoi, the great stinking vulture—and all these doves of Paradise took flight.

"Siu-lan, my sorrow did not choke me then with the intensity I feel today in telling you about it. Yes, of course I was sad. I saw those two eyes and I heard that mouth, but the little details of life—a smell, a color, a lovely carving, a woman passing—had the power to distract me then. My great sorrow was constantly interrupted by little joys.

"But now, Siu-lan, describing that memory for you, I feel for the first time the greatness of my sorrow then. A total, pure sorrow, corrupted by no joy great or small."

I stopped talking. I was deeply moved. Suddenly I felt that I would lose Siu-lan—as if such grief, suddenly so pure, was only a horrible foreboding, a preparation for my heart to receive its great loss. Already I was training my soul and my body to be able to endure.

Siu-lan looked up; from her long lashes hung a last drop of bitter dew. She looked at me a long time in silence; for a moment I thought I saw in her eyes an unexpected cruelty, a gleam of steel.

Her lips stirred. For a second they froze into a mocking smile and I heard the whisper of her voice that sounded different to me now: "And the geishas?"

"I'm sorry," I said; "I had forgotten them."

"I hadn't!" Siu-lan answered in a new, incisive tone.

26

*T*HEN I SHALL obey you, Siu-lan!

"While I was wandering disconsolately through the temple of Kwannon, I ran into my Japanese friend Kuge. The schoolmaster was as emaciated as ever, his complexion deep yellow, his huge eyes flaming. I have always been very fond of him, for he dares say 'I' and in this little word includes all his race. I loved him for his ardent purity, his cruel youth and for the insolence of his claims.

"As soon as he caught sight of me in the crowd, alone and at loose ends, he ran toward me. 'What's the matter with you, O demon from the ocean?' he exclaimed, shaking me by the shoulder. 'My poor friend, how strange you look. What has happened to you in this land of camouflaged cannons?'

"I told him of my descent into the 'City of Suffering.'

" 'Come now,' he said, 'you must not leave Japan with this bitter memory. Come with me tonight. You shall see different women, purer than your virgins, innocent and delightful as gazelles. And women who know how to smile.'

" 'I'm tired of masks!' I exclaimed, exasperated.

" 'What masks?'

" 'You know, the Japanese faces. All of them, men and women, smile like masks. And you never know what face is hidden behind the mask. I want to see a real face of warm flesh, laughing or crying or even insulting me—it wouldn't matter! But no mask!'

" 'But there is no mask, O White Barbarian! Or if you prefer, there is no face! If you strip off the mask you speak of, you shall find another exactly like the first. And if you strip off that second mask you will find another, and another, and still another to infinity! But enough of these vain words; it's getting late, the lanterns are lit. Come on!'

" 'Kuge-san,' I said, 'don't walk so fast! Let us take leave of the old Japan slowly. Take pity on it, dear friend. Give it one loving glance. It is dying. . . .'

"Kuge laughed.

" 'Among us, anyone who dies returns to the sacred reservoir of the ancestors and becomes a god. Why then take pity on the dying? There is no death. Death is a Western invention.'

"Kuge fell silent a moment; he struggled with his hollow, tubercular cough. I watched him and was touched with pity. 'He'll die soon,' I told myself, 'he'll die soon.'

" 'The old Japan is not dying,' my friend continued, very pale now. 'It's not dying, it's rejuvenating. We're grafting new variations onto our old stock. Allow me to reveal to you, dear White Man, the three most characteristic features of our soul which seems so enigmatic to you: the Japanese soul readily accepts foreign ideas; it does not accept them slavishly—it assimilates them; once assimilated, it indissolubly reintegrates them with its own traditions and everything becomes homogeneous once again.'

"Suddenly Kuge stopped. A quiet alley. Two big red lanterns. Under the lanterns, an open door. We walked in. A tiny courtyard, the cobblestones freshly washed. Two cherry trees blooming in porcelain pots; in a white marble basin floated a few yellow flowers.

"Three young girls appeared, their faces mischievous and smiling; they bowed deeply and the little courtyard was filled with their cooing voices.

" 'Irasshaimase! Irasshaimase! Welcome!'

"They removed our shoes, slipped soft leather scuffs on our feet and went before us to show us the way. We climbed a large staircase of scented wood.

"The staircase was high, the young women beautiful, the odor sweet, and suddenly I felt happy. A simple, pure happiness, the trivial ecstasy that does not trouble the senses but that spirits away the frontiers between body and soul—a transparent intoxication consisting of perfumes, smiles, and the promise of love.

"A bare room: delicate matting, a brazier, cushions. Hanging on the bamboo wall, a *kakemono:* Buddha, pot-bellied and astride a buffalo, threw back his head and laughed. Between his fleshy fingers he was holding a big blue flower.

"We sat cross-legged beside the brazier with its glowing coals. We were served green tea and rice cakes; then roasted pistachio nuts and a flat bottle of sake.

"I drank the warm sake, nibbled the pistachio nuts, and thought how love can be a gentle, chaste joy without the complications of morality, without any Christian or Romantic sentimentalism. The three geishas crouching beside us glanced up, smiling, and waited for a sign.

" 'Kuge-san,' I said to my friend, 'ask the eldest, please, what was the greatest joy of her life.'

"Rather shocked by my indiscretion, my friend passed on my request; the young woman lowered her eyes.

" 'I do not remember any great joy,' she said at last, in a low voice. 'My father sold me at the age of seven. Then I began to learn how to dance, to sing, to play the *samisen* and to please men. I have had much pleasure in my life, but . . .'

"She broke off, embarrassed. She felt she had said too much.

"We asked the youngest, crouching beside me like a kitten, 'What is your greatest desire?'

"She blushed and leaned over the brazier. She remained silent. Then the eldest began to laugh bitterly.

" 'To marry. To find a man who would take her into his house. To have children. That is what we all desire!'

"A shadow of sadness spread in the room. I was touched with remorse. How many times in my life have I not forgotten Buddha's great admonition: 'Never ask a stranger his story; it is always sad; the man often forgets, but you will never forget it again!'

"The eldest geisha set the *samisen* on her knees and began to sing:

> I *have been a geisha here for long years, waiting*
> *for my love*
> And *this morning I saw in a dream that he had*
> *come;*
> I *wakened and I weep,*
> I *am weeping still!*

"The young geisha came over to me, prostrated herself until her tiny nose was flattened on the matting.

" 'She is asking your permission to dance,' my friend explained.

"The third geisha, crouching beside Kuge, perfumed, painted, silent, glowed in the dim light like a tiny illuminated temple.

"The geisha with the *samisen* continued singing:

> All *this long, long night,*
> Long *as the tail of the golden pheasant . . .*
> Must *I sleep alone?*

"The eternal cry of a woman reluctant to sleep alone. My heart melted. Another woman, thousands of years ago, voiced the same complaint on the scented shores of the Greek island: *The moon has set and the Pleiades; the night is half gone, the hour passes and I lie here alone!*

"The young geisha began dancing to the *samisen*; chaste movements, an ardent and sober expression, a feverish impatience restrained by grace. At the moment when passion was about to reach its climax she controlled herself and returned to the quivering discipline of modesty. She was miming a woman waiting for her lover.

"I watched her, transported by this marvelously balanced play of passion and grace. The wall screen slides back; Buddha, coming down from his *kakemono*, approaches the woman, takes pity on her, assumes the face of her lover. The woman gives a cry of happiness and again prostrates herself before us, her tiny nose crushed on the matting. The dance is over.

"She stands up, smiles, and crouches beside me. I hear my heart and the woman's heart, two creatures playing together on the matting—cat and mouse. Sometimes I feel I am the cat, sometimes the mouse in this subtle game. The other geisha stands up and the *samisen* begins again.

"She sings in a slightly hoarse voice:

Tatoe hi no naka mizu no soko . . .

Through fire and flood, we are united,
Man and woman, beyond death!

"The geisha flings herself into the dance. The lover has come, passion bursts forth, love overwhelms shame.

"Oysters and another bottle of sake are served. Joy brightens our faces. I begin using all the Japanese words I know: heart, cherry blossom, thank you, sun, moon, yes, no, I am happy.

"A child with laughing eyes appears on the threshold: 'The bath is ready!' she says.

"Once our bodies are refreshed, we slip on light *yukatas* and return, barefoot, to the room with the fat Buddha.

"The sound of silk tearing. Is it a kimono? Or the silk mattress being quickly spread?

"The odor of sake, oysters and rice powder dissolving sweat. . . .

"And when we get up, toward dawn, the three geishas kneel before us on the matting, as a sign of gratitude and respect.

"A melodious gong echoes through the air; someone must have come early to pray in the temple next door.

"Out in the street, I feel like a beetle sprinkled with yellow dust; he has spent the night, the heavy scarab, in a flower, and his whole body, head, legs and belly have emerged covered with pollen.

"I was happy and pure, I had conquered the nightmare of Christianity: at last I had embraced a woman without thinking of anything but a woman.

"I was pleased with my body; my body was pleased with me. And a tender and liberating *haiku* flashed through my mind:

> *"One for the other, let us have sympathy,*
> *O mountain cherry tree, O my body.*
> *Except for you, I know no one."*

I fell silent. Before the woman he desires, a man returns to animal forms—peacock, turkey, cockerel—which he supposes he has left behind forever. Before Siu-lan, I had spread all my brightest feathers to dazzle her. Neither my joy with the geishas nor my suffering at Tamanoi was actually so intense; but I had heightened the details to show off my heart and my mind.

I fell silent, abashed, and listened in our silence to the two canaries passionately singing of love.

"Yes," Siu-lan said at last, her lips pursed, as she stood up.

"Siu-lan!" I exclaimed. "No, I did not feel that night the great happiness I have described. With you beside me, facing this flower garden, I have let myself go—my words have assumed an ardor greatly in excess of the pleasures those geishas afforded me. Please forgive me!"

Siu-lan lowered her head, hesitating. She had stood up quickly in order to leave, and now she remained, undecided.

I realized that the moment was a fateful one.

"Siu-lan," I murmured, "O mountain cherry tree . . ."

A quiver ran the length of her strong and delicate body. She seemed to be moved. Desire, shame, fear—she weighed them all between her long trembling lashes.

Gradually her face grew calm, a faint smile flickered about her lips. She opened her mouth.

I waited for the crucial word, my body bent, my features strained, trembling a little.

But just at that moment a despairing cry rose from the garden. Startled, we turned around; we had forgotten the old father's presence.

"Siu-lan!" the old man called in a muffled tone. "Siu-lan!"

The girl leaped up, anxious.

I bit my lips with rage. Siu-lan was already hurrying across the garden with her tiny, hopping steps. I saw her embracing her old father, speaking to him tenderly, pouring his tea and sitting at his feet, submissive.

"Siu-lan!" I exclaimed from the depths of my anguish. "Siu-lan!" I wanted to cry out. I took several steps toward the garden, but at that moment the door behind me opened.

"My uncle Kung Ta-hen asks you to do him the honor of dining with him this evening. He has invited for your pleasure certain scholars and poets of our country."

Li-Te spoke hastily; he was carrying his bulging briefcase. His eyes were hard and cold.

"Which uncle?" I asked.

"The old mandarin you talked to that first evening, when you arrived. Do you remember? The one who answered all your questions with: 'Yes, yes, but China is eternal.'"

I remembered the old aristocrat, and the frail, proud sound of his voice rang in my ears again. How far away that was!

"I should be delighted," I answered. "You'll be coming too, won't you?"

"I'm sorry, dear friend, but I cannot. I have too much urgent work to do. If you'll excuse me now, I have to be going."

He climbed into his ricksha and disappeared.

27

I LEFT THE HOUSE with a heavy heart and lost myself in the hallucinating spectacle of Peking like a greedy insect in the labyrinth of a great orchid. Each time I emerged dazzled and weary.

The more I breathed the air of China, the thicker grew the mystery around me and the more dangerous and incomprehensible seemed the mechanism within the yellow breast.

The silkworm, the most romantic worm on earth—that is the symbol of China. Sometimes the practical and pedestrian Chinese have the gaiety and delicacy of butterflies. The poets of this realistic people have discovered unique accents to celebrate the delights of inaction and reverie.

> *Let us build our hut under the pines—*
> *And here, bareheaded, let us write poems—*
> *Heeding only the sunrise and the sunset!*

In this transmutation of fetid mud lies China's irresistible charm. Here everything is scrupulously elaborated in secret;

hatred is repressed, love is cruel—the armed smile of voracious teeth. When the Chinese humbly bows before you and submits in silence to your irritation, you shudder, for you divine that his silence consists of shrieks repressed.

Yesterday, in a teahouse, I watched with admiration as the waiter served me. I had never seen fingers so quick and skillful, a submission so intelligent and sober, an intuition so infallible. Before I could speak a word, even before I could make a gesture, he understood and produced whatever was desired.

What happiness, I thought, to have a servant so faithful and so marvelously trained! Life could become endurable.

I looked up to give him a smile of approval, but drew back, alarmed; I had surprised his gaze, which was piercing me like a dagger.

The sun set in pink and orange mists. The evening star hung in the west like a dewdrop. The reddish walls of the Forbidden City, the green and honey-yellow tiles faded slowly into the darkness.

We were on a high terrace and how simple joy was, how human, without exaltation, almost unconscious. I thought of Confucius' well-weighed words: "I know why happiness is so rare in the world: the idealists place it too high, the materialists too low. For happiness is to be found beside us at our heart's level. Happiness is not the son of heaven or of earth; it is the son of man."

"Siu-lan," I said to myself, "Siu-lan, at my heart's level, humble happiness of clay . . ."

The guests arrived, fat, smiling, with long blue or black robes and tiny obsequious gestures. Almost all were old men —fleshy lips, chubby hands, calm and smiling eyes. Old China . . .

Extreme politeness, once it is a routine, costs nothing. The three hundred rules of ceremonial, the three thousand precepts of behavior, once absorbed by dint of conscious elaboration into the unconscious, become very simple instincts.

All of these well-bred Chinese greet each other, speak to each other, and observe each other's silence with an exquisite stylization.

The jasmine tea was served, and roasted melon seeds in little saucers.

"If there were not so many melon seeds in China," says one jovial and chubby old man, "we would have had many more revolutions—nibbling calms the nerves."

The long litany of Chinese dishes begins: complicated, refined, suspect.

"Don't be afraid," Kung Ta-hen says to me with a smile. "Taste everything and don't look so closely. Be brave. Tonight we're not serving silkworm cakes, nor puppies in caterpillar sauce."

Then, pointing his delicate finger at several bottles of wine: "Try one. In this wine a young monkey has been pickled. Apparently it is very stimulating, a marvelous *apéritif* for love. In this one, only a chicken: apparently it soothes physical suffering. And in this one a snake: it is supposed to arouse strange curiosities. Choose!"

I chose the snake.

"Let us drink to your compatriot, Socrates," exclaimed an old bearded professor. "Confucius and Socrates were two masks covering the same face: the luminous, precisely-lined face of human logic."

The snake wine had no bouquet and tasted harsh.

"If we drink two more glasses of this wine," I said, "human logic will be in danger."

"So much the better!" answered an old poet with very long, gleaming nails. "It will give way to music, which is the supreme logic, and you know how our Confucius loved wine, music and women. Exactly like your Socrates."

I contemplated these old men around me with admiration, their moderate joy, their subtle smiles, their marvelously young hearts. How many times, in the middle of the street, have I not stopped to admire an old mandarin as he passed, his resplendent face calm, his disillusioned mouth smiling at all the infernal racket of the Chinese street, and his little eyes understanding and forgiving all ugliness. . . .

Kung Ta-hen clapped his hands and gave a brief order to the epicene waiter who appeared.

He was brought a pink calling card; on it the old mandarin traced several lines. "Be quick," he ordered the waiter.

And turning toward us: "With your permission, I have invited Evening Flower, our famous 'Sister of the Hearth.' She is no longer in her first youth, but she is still disturbing."

A great tray of sweets was served.

"Try them, try them!" the old poet whispered to me. "They're made of lotus; you'll forget your country."

We drank the snake wine again and the edges of things began to blur.

And suddenly a woman appeared in the middle of the terrace, noiseless as a ghost, heavily painted, her eyebrows "like the two-days' moon," her face, between the long jade earrings, as smooth as a stone on the sea floor, looking as if it had been lacquered by kisses.

Yes, her face was drawn, gradually worn by the caresses of the hands and lips of countless pilgrims. Suddenly *Porciuncola*, the little chapel of St. Francis of Assisi, came to my mind; it, too, like this woman, has been licked smooth over the centuries by the countless kisses of ardent pilgrims.

"Evening Flower!" pronounced the old mandarin gravely as he bowed.

I started. Where had I seen this woman whose face was ravaged by love? In some great crowd . . . in some remote city . . . but where?

Evening Flower sat down, spread her fan and smiled. Her eyes were long and narrow. They moved slowly and flowed over us, bestowing on each a somnolent, remote gaze. She looked like a tigress that has drunk blood and is about to yawn.

At last her lips parted, and in a whisper she began to sing some ancient melody of the desert. It was a song of the camel drivers crossing the terrible Gobi, a monotonous, insistent, despairing chant.

But where had I heard that voice?

Evening Flower finished her song and fell silent; her voice had sounded hoarse and fatigued. Her delicate hands embraced the teacup and raised it.

"I am happy," she said, smiling. "I am happy, but I can sing no more this night. Forgive me, my lords, I am a little weary."

She took from her hair and distributed among us jasmine blossoms that were warm, faded and heavily perfumed.

She turned toward me. Immediately a light flashed through my memory. Yes, I had seen her in Moscow, at a great celebration in an imperial hall of the Kremlin. She had come in the name of Red China and she had sung that evening a revolutionary song. How could I ever forget the jerky rhythm, that hoarse voice, the pitiless attack of the abrupt, foreign words that were like cries of a hungry bird of prey?

I approached Evening Flower, who had just moistened her lips in the teacup. I bowed before her. She looked up at me with a smile, but suddenly her face darkened. She lowered her eyes as if she wanted to look at the tiny Buddha crouching in the bottom of her cup.

"Have I not seen you somewhere before, O Evening Flower?" I asked her in a low voice.

"No!" she answered quickly. Then, "Where?"

"Somewhere in a distant city . . . in the snow. . . ."

She frowned.

"You must have seen me in a dream, O foreigner!" she murmured. "I trouble men's sleep sometimes," she added dryly.

She turned toward the satiated and half-drunk mandarins: "The desire has come upon me, my lords," she said, "to sing for you again, this time a new and fashionable melody. Have I your permission?"

And without waiting for an answer, she began to sing, standing this time, her eyes glowing:

> *Eat, drink, make love, O lords!*
> *What is that red bird over your heads?*
> *It is not a wound, have no fear, O my lords!*
> *It is my mouth that sings!*

"Let us drink to the beauty of Evening Flower!" I exclaimed. "Fortunate the eyes that have seen her once, twice fortunate the eyes that have seen her a second time. And the mouth that has touched her will change in the earth to a great red flower!"

As we were drinking, Evening Flower disappeared, leaving only the perfume of jasmine behind her.

"Evening Flower is beginning to fade," Kung Ta-hen murmured after a short silence. "Autumn has come!"

His voice was compassionate, even sad. He was too old to be able to mock death.

"It is woman's most succulent season. Her body is full of sap and perfume and disturbing presentiments of corruption," the old, goat-lipped poet said. "I'm very fond of such ripe fruits; they melt in the mouth. . . ."

And I was thinking with delight of the deadly breath of the woman who has sacrificed herself to an inexorable idea. Joshiro flashed before my eyes, troubled as they were by the snake wine. Tonight I trusted her, tonight I trusted the high aim of her lust! And tonight her harsh song echoed in my ears like the psalm of a holy martyr singing as she burns for her god.

Then let Evening Flower suck the marrow of these moribund old mandarins! Blessings on this woman without pity! She saps and weakens their loins and presses the flame of her lips upon their toothless mouths. Let them sink back into the earth! Let China be rejuvenated—whether by Siu-lan, by Evening Flower or by Joshiro, it matters not!

In those terrible and succulent periods when one civilization collapses and another rises, woman—blessed be she—marvelously fulfills her high mission: she kills the dying, pitilessly, quickly!

Again the old mandarin summoned the eunuch waiter and covered another pink card with mysterious signs.

"Be quick!" he ordered, and turned to us. "A shadow," he said, "has fallen over our table. With your permission, I have sent for a Siang-kon."

Kung Ta-hen looked at me and smiled. "Stay a little longer," he said. "Drink another glass of snake wine. You will feel new curiosities within you."

My neighbor the poet leaned toward me and murmured, "Siang-kon means 'little master.' It is a bittersweet fruit, highly prized in your country, too, in antiquity. Women, you see, leave behind a bitter, almost sickening aftertaste. It is then that the young boys come to our aid, tender and silent and very skillful. They dance, sing, caress and make us forget our bitterness. Kung Ta-hen is right—drink again, dear guest. Another glass of snake wine."

"To your death!" I murmured deep in my heart, and drained my glass.

A tinkle of bracelets was heard on the terrace staircase. A rustle of silk. We turned our heads; at the top of the stairs appeared a boy of about twelve, swathed in long robes of silk and gold.

His face was heavily powdered, his lips, cheeks and nails were deep red. He seemed emaciated, sad and tired, but his full lips smiled, ambiguous and perverse.

"Welcome," I said to myself with a shudder, "O little androgynous Buddha!"

28

I RETURNED to the house very late. As on every other night, Siu-lan was still up. She slept, she assured me, only at dawn. She worked, wrote letters, filed reports, helped her brother. Her eyes, very tired, had blue circles beneath them.

This evening, too, she served me a cup of tea. She bowed in silence and withdrew. I followed the sharp tapping of her footsteps, and briefly glimpsed her hips swaying in the darkness.

For the first time I realized the mysterious charm of that barbarous mutilation of the feet: that uncertain gait, those arms held out from the body, that slight inclination of the body almost abandoning itself to chance, subtly suggesting the hesitation, the distress and wavering steps of love.

I threw myself on my bed and thought of Siu-lan as one thinks of a distant region bristling with an impenetrable flora. In her gaze, in her indistinct movements, in the suave odor of cloves that emanated from her body, there was the mystery of the musky creature that comes and goes like some hieratic cat, keeping watch over the house.

To live with such a woman, full of silence and regard, with hands so delicate and promising, with gestures so submissive and yet so proud and sure—what enrichment of everyday life!

Penetrating her secrets, I would have penetrated immemorial and immense China, her mountains, her deserts, her rivers and her perfumed forests. Deep in this young girl's carefully hidden breast stirred all the dangerous and fascinating fauna of the yellow soul—complicated legends, golden dragons, jade birds, spring dances to unknown instruments, magical incantations:

> *Upon this ceremonial day, in this propitious hour*
> *Respectfully I desire to unite myself with your*
> *   body;*
> *I bear the long sword with a jade handle,*
> *My pendants sing ling-lang;*
> *I offer a cup of wine brewed with pepper and*
> *   ginger!*
> *Raise the banners, beat the drums,*
> *Ring the bells, blow the flutes!*
> *I respectfully desire to enter your body!*

The night left empty-handed, the day returned. Ironic and hesitating at the touch of love, my heart had recovered its long-lost virginity; again it became timid and trembling and full of modesty. It desired, yet avoided the thing desired; it swelled with ardent cries yet emitted only muffled words; it had again become the plaything of an unsuspected childhood.

That day, at table, I felt Siu-lan's long stare upon me. I felt it search me like a hand. I was able to govern my agitation and raised my head; I had time to surprise a strange suffering in her great almond-shaped eyes.

"Siu-lan," I said, to justify my insistent stare, "Siu-lan, you look tired. Perhaps you do not sleep enough."

Siu-lan, speechless, lowered her eyes. Li-Te came to her rescue: "Our sons and our grandsons," he said, "may have time to sleep. They, at least, will be liberated."

"Liberated from whom?"

Li-Te hesitated a moment. "From the white men," he answered at last. "Dear friend, forgive me. From the white men and from . . . other yellow men."

"And what if they are not? Then all this insomnia will have been in vain, and the game lost. The game—that is, life, this single opportunity!"

I dared not look at Siu-lan, to whom these words were secretly addressed. But I saw Li-Te's brows pucker with irritation.

"To fight for freedom," he answered dryly, "is already to be free. Some of us in China, a small elite, are free. And the game is won."

The tone of these words sounded a little aggressive to me. Li-Te had made an instinctive movement, as if he sought to interpose himself between Siu-lan and me.

I raised my head again, ready for combat. "Yes, I know," I said, "the elite always wins. Even if it is beaten, especially if it is beaten; for only then does its virtue remain pure—I mean unrewarded. To fight for a cause you know is lost: that is the only fight worthy of a proud man."

Li-Te clenched his fists; his upper lip trembled, showing his white teeth. Li-Te was like a dog about to bite.

"We are not fighting for a lost cause!" he said, and his voice was low. "Your pure virtue is an old maid; she prides herself on having remained a virgin, her womb immaculate. We hate old maids!"

"Yes, I know," I retorted. "You are a practical man; you want to receive the wages of your efforts—to turn your virtue into small change."

"Our small change," Li-Te exclaimed, "is called the Freedom of China!"

"Still, it's just as much a reward. It's a deal—a good deal, perhaps; you are investing the capital of your personality to advantage. Hero or martyr, my dear Li-Te, you will have your reward: glory, a statue, a little legend."

"What do you want, then? To plead lost causes at any cost?"

"No, but to be more modest when you serve a lucrative cause."

And Siu-lan? I exclaimed to myself. Renounce Siu-lan? No reward? And all this regal unfolding of interior wings? Not even a cry to betray the proud joy of renunciation?

Siu-lan, pleading, touched her brother's fist.

"Brother," she said in a low voice, "look at father—don't you see how pale he is! He must be suffering. Speak to him, please."

The old mandarin, sitting in his ancestral armchair with its frieze of dragons, thrust the long ivory wands into his dish without enthusiasm. He was not hungry. He sighed, watching his son on his left, his daughter on his right, and me before him, with a distracted and pensive gaze.

"He understands everything," I told myself, "this fat, numb old man: the struggle between him and his son, between his son and me, between himself and me. And Siu-lan remains in the middle—hesitant, torn, supplicating."

In moments of weakness or kindness I made up my mind to leave—to relax this overcharged atmosphere a little, to soften fate a little; but the joy of the struggle prevailed. I would stay, to fight, to wrest this young body with its intoxicating and subtle odor, this silent and proud soul, from these two men.

Love for a woman of another race is poignant, plagued by profound curiosities, lacerated by mysterious regrets for some high treason. The more one leaves the straight and narrow path, the sweeter the temptation, the greater the promises. The danger of losing our way increases, but the circle of our experiences widens and the hope of transcending ourselves mounts. And is that not what life, that adventuress of the highroads, desires?

Let us enter her snare eyes open! Let us try to enjoy the

bait without letting the trap close over us! Let us enrich our soul by embracing, caressing matter. Mind is not made with mind, but always with the flesh!

Siu-lan is a body marvelously suited to my desires. . . . Siu-lan alone can appease the ancestral thirst of my flesh. . . . Her vibrant silence, her gracious and reticent gestures, her words full of ardor and wisdom. Siu-lan, the flower of this great yellow earth—there is salvation.

At last to be rid of white women, presumptuous, shameless, filling the air with futile or provocative noise; to rediscover the silent roots of being!

Christianity has made love into a complicated disease. By covering it with shame, it has forced us to repress and distort these simple and sacred gestures. To free oneself of this Judaic tare, to return with simplicity and gratitude to the two impeccable columns that sustain life—to man and to woman!

Li-Te stared at his old father; he managed to control his vexation. In a tender tone, he addressed a few words to the old man.

The old mandarin shrugged his shoulders and his voice rose, grave and weary. "China is sick," he said. "I, too, feel that I am sick, like my country. O white lord, kindly excuse me."

Li-Te translated these words for me, adding, "Yes, please excuse him; my father is dying of his deep wound. We are all suffering, but he is too old to react by taking action. He folds his hands; he takes refuge in the Four Books of Wisdom and smokes his long pipe in the evening in order to fall asleep. . . ."

A moment later he added in a low voice: "That is the old China; it is dying."

A heavy silence fell over the table.

Li-Te and I regretted the violent words we had just exchanged; we secretly tried to find an occasion to make it up to each other. He did not like me, I could tell; but he was polite.

166

"Siu-lan," I said, to break this heavy silence, "Siu-lan, your brother has been good enough to offer to take me into the Forbidden City. Would you come with us?"

A sudden blush colored her cheeks. "My father would not allow it," she murmured.

"Let us emancipate ourselves from Father, Siu-lan," her brother said in a tender and firm tone of voice. "Let us follow our own road, my sister. Come!"

The old mandarin stood up at this moment, clasped his hands, bowed and withdrew. Siu-lan, with her dancing steps, ran after him; every day, she went to light his long pipe for him and serve his tea. She took him tenderly by the arm and they slowly disappeared behind the door with its intricate old carvings.

"Siu-lan," Li-Te murmured, "understands everything, but she is only a woman; you must forgive her."

And after a moment's reflection: "Forgive her and help her, willy-nilly, but tenderly toward . . . the right path. A woman's development is slow; she must be trained, even forced a little."

At this moment Siu-lan reappeared; she served us tea.

"Siu-lan," Li-Te resumed, "you will come with us, won't you?"

Siu-lan did not answer. She poured out our tea and stared out the window at the swarming street—rickshas, coolies, strolling peddlers, beggars, gold-lettered signs, a robust girl dancing at the corner and her old mother crouching beside her, tapping a tambourine.

A vague murmur reached our ears and irreverently penetrated even into this venerable dining room with its old empty ancestors' armchairs.

"Siu-lan," her brother insisted.

"Yes," Siu-lan answered, and lowered her head. Her voice trembled a little; two great tears had suddenly appeared at the corners of her darkened eyes.

I took pity on her suffering. I understood the struggle that was being waged in her being; her intelligence was in agreement with her brother: to free herself of the old traditions, to let the dead rot in their graves at last, to acknowledge that the living had the right and the duty to live. . . .

Yes, Siu-lan understood everything; her intelligence, thanks to her pitiless brother, gentle as he was toward her, was freed at last; but her heart, her poor loving heart remained still enslaved; it lingered beside the old father.

Li-Te caught sight of the huge furtive tears and stiffened. He was jealous of the sway his father continued to exercise over Siu-lan's heart. Li-Te felt a secret animosity toward him, an unconscious hatred. He often glanced at the heavy mass of the old arthritic Buddha and anger rose in his eyes; anger, melancholy, and fear, too—as if he saw all China in his father, wizened and weak as he was. How transform this slack and shuffling mass into a spearhead of steel? The sight of his father sometimes made him shudder. Would they ever achieve victory? Would the attempts to liberate this enormous, benumbed mass be unrealizable and insane?

Here in his own house, he had not succeeded in completely liberating his own sister. The old man disputed over her with him at each step.

"Siu-lan," I said, trying to control the tenderness that suddenly flooded me. "Siu-lan, if it gives you pain, I do not insist!"

"No, no, Siu-lan will come!" her brother interrupted again, rather abruptly. "Siu-lan struggles, and each step she takes forward costs her something, but she takes it. Siu-lan is our new China. If she succumbs, we are lost!"

Siu-lan raised her eyes. This role her brother attributed to her burdened her with responsibility and pride. Siu-lan incarnated the new China; how then could she compromise her race? To suffer and conquer—to suffer horribly and conquer—that was her destiny.

"Yes," she said, in a determined voice, and tiny drops gleamed at the tips of her long lashes; "yes, my brother, I shall come."

29

*T*HIS IS THE Forbidden City!" murmured Li-Te,
gesturing toward the arcades and the powerful roofs
with their gilded horns and green tiles. "Here lies exotic
China, fit for the tourists."

This tone of banter outraged my heart. I turned toward
Siu-lan, as if to ask her help; but she was already crossing
the sacred threshold, a trifle pale, her eyes lowered.

"Let us be on our guard," I told myself, "and restrain our
outcry. Let us contemplate beauty in silence."

Vague forebodings oppressed me; the alternating shadows
of love and death brightened and darkened my soul. Until
dawn, I had stared out the open window as the night passed,
transparent and blue, and inhaled with a pained sensuality
the smell of the freshly spaded earth in the garden.

Now I climbed the magnificent marble stairs, and a tremendous miracle flowered before my eyes. Red, green, blue
palaces disintegrated gently under the breeze; I picked up bits
of the colored plaster and crumbled them between my fingers.
I felt the ashes of ancient lust cover me like pollen.

I walked slowly and cast around me "the glance of the elephant" that Buddha recommended to his disciples:

See all things as if it were for the first time;
See all things as if it were for the last time!

I greeted and took my leave of all things. With my left hand—for the other was clenched with indignation and grief —I caressed the marble, the gates, the wood carvings, the wild plants.

Old China is passing, the paint falls from her faded cheeks and her tapering fingers are gnawed by leprosy; only her jade rings still remain. . . .

Li-Te, behind me, tapped the stones with his slender bamboo cane; he did not speak, but I sensed how nervous and tense he was. I wanted to force him to speak; I could not endure this hostile silence any longer.

"Praised be luxury!" I exclaimed in a provocative tone; "what we call superfluous luxury, the peacock's plume! That is what civilization is: to feel that luxury is as indispensable as bread; to aspire to something beyond food, sleep and love. Life is a woman; she proceeds by loving, expending without calculation, raising luxury to its true place: the sacred place of necessity. A work of beauty counts more than a work of goodness, of truth, or of justice. Why? No one knows.

"Your Confucius, the supreme flower of common sense, has said: 'The king is like the wind; the people are like the grass. When the wind passes, the grass must bow.' What has happened? The wind has passed, the grass has passed too, but the beautiful phrase remains."

"Yes . . ." Siu-lan began, moved, and she leaned against a bronze stork. But she broke off at once, noticing that her brother's hand was clenched into a fist.

"You are a poet," Li-Te said sarcastically. "Your heart, so tender in appearance, is dry and cruel, like the hearts of all artists. You do not think of human suffering, but of the expression on men's faces and the intonations of their cries

170

when they suffer. We men of action, hard as we appear, when we see a man or a people suffer, suffer with them. More: we fight to put an end to their suffering!

"I hate beauty because it dries up hearts and pours out an inhuman poison for us to drink: oblivion."

I listened to this explosion with a carefully concealed joy. Li-Te must have been too nervous today to control himself; I had caught him at a moment of weakness and I was taking advantage of it. Finally he had let me glimpse a bit of his soul.

He turned, saw me listening greedily for his words, and immediately checked himself.

"Forgive me, dear friend," he murmured. "I was carried away. But China is not a beautiful painted corpse. She is alive, and she suffers. Do you not understand?"

I did not answer. Yes, I understood. All this yellow skin, at the least touch, screams with rage and pain, tormented by an inferiority complex. Its nerves are laid bare.

We walked on in silence. I wanted to fling myself into the arms of this wounded brother, but I held myself back. I knew how suspect my sudden gesture of kindness was in his eyes, and any effusion, to him as well as to me, seemed degrading.

I looked at my friend out of the corners of my eyes and admired him in silence. I thought of the Japanese samurais who went off to war in their heavy steel armor; but between it and their skin they wore a delicate silk shirt. And when they fell on the battlefield, in their helmet or in the folds of their belt was found some inexplicably tender verse:

> O plum tree before my house,
> I shall never return,
> But you do not forget to blossom
> Again in the spring!

Siu-lan hopped like a shepherdess from one stone to the next. Around her the temples were crumbling to dust, the weeds were overgrowing the gods. The palaces, having survived their little fever of life, were gently returning to nothingness.

For a moment Siu-lan turned back and smiled at me; I thought I saw the ruins covered with wild violets.

A blind, blood-colored wall rose before us. At its top gleamed huge white characters in relief; they intertwined, unraveled and bleached in the sun like tiny skeletons of women, like human skulls, vertebrae and tibiae.

"The imperial gynaeceum," Siu-lan murmured.

The sun was overcast; a few drops of rain fell on our cheeks, large and warm as tears. A strange calm. A bittersweet sensation, an intoxication of earth, as distant flashes of mute, pale blue lightning appeared and vanished again, flickering over the treetops.

For a moment I looked down and felt the Buddha's grace descend upon me, licking my eyelids and temples like a tongue.

I opened my eyes and saw Siu-lan leaning over a pond, looking at the reflection of her face. Once it had been a stream that joyously rippled under the white marble bridge; today it was a stagnant black pool.

I leaned, too, and saw my crude face beside her delicate and beautiful one. Both were reflected, quivering. . . . I shuddered; this pool suddenly seemed to me like the gentle and pitiless eye of Buddha. The two wretched faces united in death, lost in the depths of a black pupil. . . . I had the overpowering sense that life was short and that we had no time to be timid or moral.

Siu-lan straightened, and her face disappeared from the surface of the water—I remained alone.

"The imperial gynaeceum . . ." she repeated.

I stood up and Siu-lan pointed at the red wall and the macabre characters on it.

"Siu-lan," I said, noticing how pale her face was, "you are tired."

"No," she answered. "Let's go up!"

Li-Te had found a miserable kitten, some descendant of the huge imperial cats, and was caressing it as he sat on the marble bridge.

Cats were once doted on in these palaces of decadence; when the empress' favorite cat gave birth, the courtiers sent her presents: silk ribbons, silver bells, tiny mice on gold plates.

"Go on up," Li-Te said with a shrug. "I'll wait for you here. Forgive me, but I loathe dead beauties. I prefer this cat."

Silk, ivory, amber and pearl exert a mysterious charm upon the human soul, the human skin. From head to toe, our skin rejoices when we look at these precious substances or even think of them with our eyes closed. That is why silk, ivory, amber and pearl have played a capital role in the ennobling of the human senses and in love—that is, in civilization.

I saw these objects of luxury and lust displayed in the cases of the gynaeceum like little naked corpses: fans, earrings, bracelets, mirrors; tiny oil lamps which, one tragic night, were extinguished forever; hard porcelain pillows on which were painted women weeping under the willows.

To see all these secret objects with Siu-lan next to me filled my heart with an ineffable pain and desire. I smelled the musky odor of pepper—of pepper and faded roses that this virgin body beside me exhaled.

"Siu-lan," I said. I was gasping for breath and my lips trembled.

"No, no!" she said, frightened, and she clung to one of the cases with the dead lamps inside. Her eyes were filled with terror, but her lips smiled, pale now.

"Are you afraid, Siu-lan?" I asked, breathing hard. "Are you afraid?"

"Yes," she murmured, and her great black eyes flickered in anguish, like a gazelle at bay.

Suddenly I took pity on her. What is this shameless mystery, then, that we call love? In the void, I see nothing. Nothing but a black wing that brushes against us as it passes.

"Siu-lan," I said, "I shall not speak. Please don't be afraid."

"Thank you," she murmured, and the smile vanished from her lips.

30

I STROLLED ALONE from alcove to alcove, and caressed a long series of shadows. Yellow emperors, yellow empresses, human annals written on water. . . .

Only a fervent heart that remembers and loves can still give its blood to these shadows and restore them to life—fill again the doors, the windows, the stairs with warm bodies.

"I declare war on time! I declare war on time!" the heart cries, and turns the wheel back and resuscitates the dead.

The emperor, a great doll heavy with gold and jewels, rises out of the earth. He is borne from one pavilion to the other, depending on the season. In spring, dressed in green, he eats grain and lamb; in summer, dressed in red, he is fed green beans and chicken; in autumn, dressed in white silk, he eats dog; in winter, dressed in black, he eats millet and pork . . .

And every evening he comes here to his gynaeceum to visit his wives. Ten thousand wives—they lie in wait for the passing of his chariot drawn by lambs—and each holds out a crumb of salt to attract the lambs to herself alone. . . .

Refinement, barbarism, man's superhuman effort to achieve an eternal work—and suddenly there sprouts upon this yellow earth, by the collaboration of all, a great human tree with its olive-like fruit: Confucius.

Active virtue, utilitarian morality, order, submission and politeness, good sense that measures all things.

But then, above this commonplace genius, leaps into the air the great dragon of the mystical Tao, Lao-tse. Confucius stares at it, dazzled: *I know that fish swim; I know that birds fly; but the power of the Dragon I cannot measure.*

Lao-tse is the superior stage of Confucius, the higher level of action and virtue. The divine madness, the disappearance into the All, the supreme virtue with folded arms.

Sancho and Don Quixote, the eternal pillars of the world. The intense coexistence of such divergent elements creates the rich civilization of China. Without the solid and practical intervention, the contact with the Tao would remain confused and shapeless. Without the mystical impulse, reason would remain sterile, incapable of desiring and consequently of realizing great things superior to immediate necessity.

Here, too, the two great leaders, Don Quixote and Don Sancho, collaborating, have created the visible and the invisible world. . . .

I heard tiny, hopping footsteps; I turned around and saw Siu-lan coming toward me, her eyes enormous, filling her listless face.

"Siu-lan," I said, "look at these dilapidated palaces and these weeds; life is short, take pity on it!"

She let her eyes flicker over the tent-shaped roofs, over the blue, green and yellow tiles; tall sharp-leaved weeds swayed along the cornices, gradually displacing the tiles and the beams. And below, on the imperial pavement uprooted by weeds, strolled the tourists and the crows.

Siu-lan sighed. She opened her lips that were so fond of silence, but said nothing.

"Yes, Siu-lan," I continued gently so as not to startle her, "I have wandered through the ruins of great human efforts all over the world. Ephemeral man's desperate assaults on immortality have always filled my soul with admiration and pity.

"Perhaps you do not know, Siu-lan, about one of the greatest leaders of the white race: Don Quixote. He is a knight-errant, intrepid and whimsical, who hurls himself into the wildest adventures, without arms, without friends and without hope. Beaten, he begins again; spat upon, he exults; deceived, he curls his gray mustache and triumphantly re-enters the trap. In his agony, he flings the gauntlet at his supreme enemy and dies denying death.

"Our Lord Don Quixote is one of the great leaders of the white race—and of the yellow race as well. We serve, Siu-lan, in the same army, and I am glad of it. And you, Siu-lan?"

I held out my hand, and with my fingertips I touched her left shoulder. Instinctively, to transmit an idea to a woman, an irresistible force inspired me to touch her body lightly. As if woman were forever incapable of grasping an abstract idea, it must be offered to her enveloped in warm flesh.

I felt Siu-lan shudder. For a moment her eyelids flickered like wounded wings.

And suddenly the long series of paintings in vernal colors that I had glimpsed in these palaces passed before my eyes, flooded with desires that brooded over Siu-lan.

Streams with tender reeds, gold fish, tiny boats filled with young women, trees with flame flowers, like gentle, motion-less conflagrations . . . A girl brings a basket of wisteria to Buddha, who is sitting on the grass; she fixes her suppliant eyes upon him without opening her heavy, sensual lips. What is the use of words? He knows well, that great Shep-herd of human illusions, the unspoken cry of all young girls.

Suddenly everything vanished; and on the blue canvas of the air a painting trembled, its colors brilliant; an old ancestor smiles, crouching on a great wild rock. Beside him, a golden pheasant contemplates, like a king, the enormous snow-covered landscape. A faint intoxication fills the mind; the refined heart no longer cries out; the ascetic stares far off, through a light mist, at all the beloved forms of earth as they appear, distinct for a moment, and then gently dissolve into the mist.

I drew my hand away; before me I saw again the great deserted courtyards, the granite lions, the winged dragons, the marble terraces, and the porches, the columns, the lintels, carved over and over again with the two eternal symbols of human effort: the Cloud and the Flame.

A great flame, a desperate passion, has brought all these marvels into being—palaces, paintings, red lips, great ideas, magnanimous actions. It has gone up in smoke and sways an instant above our heads, like a cloud.

Why? I stare at these luxuriant and abandoned ruins, I look, close beside me, at this young woman's body with its voluptuously swelling breasts and I can barely contain a wild cry. In the flicker of an eyelash I feel beauty—whether a whole civilization or a frail woman—rising from the earth, blooming in the empty air and falling back to earth. I hear the joints of my skull cracking. But I manage to check my hand which ardently sought to feel again the quivering of that young shoulder.

"Let's go back down," Siu-lan murmured in a pleading tone. "Li-Te is waiting."

Siu-lan went ahead of me; her tiny feet in their goatskin clogs gently brushed against the staircase of the wives and the eunuchs. From repressing the sudden movements of my desire, my arms and knees felt terribly tired. I murmured:

> *O great square which has no corners,*
> *Great vase forever incomplete,*
> *Great voice which forms no words,*
> *Great appearance without form—*
> *O desire!*

31

*L*i-Te was speaking in low tones to a stocky Chinese; his face was radiant. The man, bending forward humbly, was answering his urgent questions.

As soon as they heard us approaching, both stopped talking and turned toward us. I started; I had immediately recognized the lame man with the scar across his forehead!

"I'll be leaving you," Li-Te said in a pleased tone. "I have to get on with my work. Let's be on our way," he whispered to his companion. "We have no time to waste!"

Siu-lan started with alarm; she began to make a gesture, as if she had wanted to stretch out her arms and restrain her brother; her lips stirred as if they were about to cry out: "Don't leave us alone!"

But already Li-Te, with his elastic strides, was passing through the great gate. The man followed him, vigilant. He was no longer limping; his body seemed robust and supple now.

"Joshiro!" I murmured, shuddering. My heart stood still. "Joshiro must be in some danger. . . ."

And at that moment I realized how dear to me that ugly and cruel woman was. She, too, was fighting in the decimated but resolute army of a great warrior. Checking her implacable pain, she followed the traces of his blood.

She gave this Great Warrior another name; she gave another goal to the battle. But, beyond the divergent appearances, we were both fighting, Joshiro and I, side by side. She didn't know it; but I knew, and I loved her as the soldier loves his comrade.

"Joshiro is in danger . . . Joshiro is in danger . . ." I murmured.

A fine spring rain began falling again; the choking air grew cool. The earth exhaled a gentle odor and the palaces sank into a tender mist.

A strange impatience seized my body. Let us make haste! Life is short, only a moment; we must not let the moment perish, colorless and empty! What is our duty? To transform the moment into eternity.

The ruins of the palaces, the cemeteries, the spring shower, the smell of the turned earth—all give us their great advice: "O ephemeral shadows, make haste!"

And the memory of Joshiro lashed my heart.

"Siu-lan," I said, "we are alone now. What is the thing you love most in Peking? Let us go and see it!"

A sudden alarm flickered over her ivory countenance, but she braved the danger.

"Let us go, then," she said, and it was as if she were staking her life on this insignificant decision.

She called the coolies and we climbed into our rickshas. The coolies' soles clapped softly against the moist earth— flowering acacias, wisteria, peonies. . . . We crossed a great garden; its suave perfumes covered all the stench of China.

Ancient dwarf trees, a cherry tree in a pot covered with blossoms—I felt an unexpected uneasiness, as if I were seeing a little girl pregnant. In the garden's greenish pond danced red and blue fish.

A litany of camels with velvet eyes; they crossed Peking like a desert.

Siu-lan, leaning back in her ricksha, glided ahead, and I, suddenly spurred on with fierce happiness, pursued her from street to street through the crowd that parted to let us pass.

We crossed the narrow Street of the Fans, the Street of the Lanterns, the Street of Jade; we passed the mysterious shops where love potions are sold. The human swarm stirred in the moist, gentle light.

"To have eyes and ears," I mused, "what happiness! To see, to hear this splendid fantasy, the world. To run from the cradle to the grave, glancing greedily right and left!"

Siu-lan turned around; she smiled, very pale; the raindrops sprinkled her face like tears.

"Here it is," she said, pointing to a great stone staircase.

Siu-lan looked tired; we climbed slowly. Leaning toward her, I avidly, discreetly inhaled her body.

When, for the first time, I came into contact with this yellow race, I had experienced an invincible corporeal repugnance. And now this young and perfumed body had demolished all barriers, merely by sighing. Was it love, desire, or simply a woman's warm odor that had helped me understand?

One of these nights, sleeping in her father's house, I had had a dream; surely if her breath and her perfume were not spread in the air I breathed, such a dream would never have illuminated and enlarged my heart:

The earth was covered with mulberry leaves; on these leaves crawled masses of silkworms, slowly, greedily nibbling. A gigantic man emerged from among this vermin and cast great handfuls of mulberry leaves over these silkworms. . . .

"Eat everything," he murmured, "eat everything."

It was clear that this giant was eager to make these worms pass quickly through the whole circle of their evolution . . . to drive them to the supreme stage of the silkworm: the white butterfly.

For a moment the giant turned around and smiled at me;

I slowly bowed my head, for I had recognized him: it was Buddha.

Oh, the long pilgrimage through those silkworms, lasting the whole night! That slow rustle of the working mouths, of the bodies that entwined, sprawling in their heaps of ordure. . . . And suddenly the silk they excreted and the winged spirit rising up from them!

From that night on I had begun to see the whole circle—the mulberry leaf, the ordure, the silk. I was beginning to understand China.

"Siu-lan," I said, touching my guide's hand lightly, "Siu-lan, I thank you. . . ."

We were already at the top of the stairs, in a little garden. Siu-lan turned around, surprised. "For what?" she asked. And without waiting for an answer she slipped into the little temple that appeared before us between the trees.

Gentle, perfumed dimness; I entered behind Siu-lan, stumbling in the darkness.

"What is it?" I whispered. "I can't see a thing."

"Do not speak!" she implored. At that moment someone crouching in the shadows stood up. I distinguished an old priest in his orange robe. He extended one hand and a light came on. I could scarcely keep from exclaiming, for, in front of us, deep in a niche, was a hallucinating apparition—Buddha!

He was in the flower of his youth, very tender, with long, disturbing eyes, and the smile radiated from all his body of precious stone.

Never did any statue communicate to me so intense a joy; no, it was not joy, it was liberation; the freedom, the proud sensation that I had finally rid myself of the loathsome ego, that I had demolished the barriers of body, soul and thought, and that I was leaping forward to lose myself at last—or to find myself—in the transparent immensity of the void.

I felt I was swimming noiselessly, slowly, as though in a dream, in green and transparent waters, by moonlight. For the first time I had understood Buddha's doctrine. What is nirvana? Absolute annihilation, or the eternal union with the Universe? Down through the centuries theologians and scholars have argued over this insoluble problem. You see this Buddha of jade, and your mind is filled with certainty. You *live* nirvana. Neither annihilation nor immortality! Time and space disappear; the problem changes form, it achieves its highest expression which transcends human speech. You can only live it; you hold it quite simply by living it.

You see this young Buddha and your body is refreshed, your mind is immobilized, calm for a moment above the abyss. Until this moment, the flame of this mind trembled with every wind: passions, interests, glory, beloved faces, fatherland, ideas. You see this Buddha and the flame is gradually extinguished; it is not extinguished: it becomes Buddha.

I stood a long time, lost at this mysterious center of the world. I felt that in this phosphorescent body were concentrated all the rays of the earth.

A rustle of silk; I turned around. Siu-lan was bowing deeply before her God. She rested her forehead on the cool tiles; she stood up and clapped her hands three times, as if she were calling Buddha. I had often heard the beggars, standing on the threshold, clapping their hands and asking for alms.

Siu-lan's lips stirred. She was doubtless asking her God for alms. Then she fell silent, staring at Buddha.

"Siu-lan," I said in a whisper, taking her hand.

She turned toward me, very calm now; it was as if she were expecting my gesture and my words.

"Siu-lan, would you like us to make our way together toward this jade nothingness?"

I felt her hand trembling in my palm like a tiny captive bird.

"Siu-lan . . ."

But she remained deep in her Buddha; I felt she was

183

happy, leaping, dancing like a plume of seaweed in the deep waters of Buddha.

She had heard my words, but she was in no hurry to reply. Time was abolished in her heart, it was transformed into a mute music.

"Siu-lan . . ."

She turned; her face gleamed like a pebble from the sea.

"Yes," she whispered, and she lowered her eyes

When we left the temple, the sun was already setting; the air had taken on green and golden tints. The rain had stopped, and in the western sky lingered blood-spattered clouds. In the east rose, enormous and deep red, silent and sad, the full moon.

I leaned against the trunk of a tree to give my heart time to grow calm. Siu-lan picked some little yellow flowers in silence.

Suddenly I distinguished in the middle of the garden a huge pedestal of variegated marble—green, mauve, white and pink. I moved toward it. A furious hunt was carved upon it—boars, dogs, horses—a frenzied activity. Once it had been the pedestal of the jade Buddha. But the temple was too small; they had been separated.

Now this pedestal stands in the middle of the garden, and above it there is only the shapeless air, empty and bluish—the last, definitive statue of Buddha, sculptured in the imperishable void.

32

*T*HIS ORIENTAL GOD without body and without soul, this mocking smile that vanished into air and filled the void with a shudder of wings, fought all night against my own God, who was burdened with a body and a soul, spattered with mud, lacerated with wounds.

All of Buddha's flesh has realized his highest ambition: it has become spirit, it has been evaporated into the void. Buddha holds on his open hand the round blue air. The Nothing; the Universe.

Buddha, that huge silkworm, has nibbled the whole mulberry tree of the world, he has eaten everything, drunk everything, embraced everything; he no longer seeks to eat, to drink, to embrace. He has come the full circle of the miracle, he takes his leave.

But my God is still hungry, still thirsty; he sees bread, wine, women, and he roars. He seeks, in sweat and blood, to transform a little flesh into spirit. I feel him in my entrails, leaving within me, from my loins to my heart, from my heart to my head, a red track.

He does not play, he cannot smile, he suffers. He believes in matter, and in tears; he touches and inhales Siu-lan's body and finds it sweet, warm, perfumed. He knows that life exists and he loves it; he knows that death exists, and struggles against death, trembling a little.

He hates the esthete's game, ironic silence, skeptical nonchalance and tolerance. He hates the minor virtues—prudence, politeness, pity, justice. He hates the supreme smile, Buddha. He is the anti-Buddha.

All night long, eyes open, I sought to catch a glimpse of his face. Toward dawn, in a flash, I had the violent vision of the Unknown. But in a flash, too, the vision disappeared and I fell back into darkness.

I appealed to that great sorceress, speech. I dropped her line into the invisible, and pulled it up again. Pale weeds, small fry, a few iridescent shellfish which, once taken from the great mysterious sea, lose their colors and turn to lead in my hands. . . .

That is all I have been able to save. Let my brothers in anguish cast them back into their souls and grant them anew both their freedom and their luster!

THE VISION

You heard the Cry and set forth. From battle to battle you passed through all the war service of militant man.

Suddenly all races moved with you, the holy army of man was arranged for battle behind you, and all earth resounded like a military encampment.

You climbed to a high peak from which the plan of battle branched out amid the coils of your brain, and all opposing expeditions united in the secret encampment of your heart.

Behind you the plants and animals were organized like supply troops for the front-line battling armies of man.

Now entire Earth clings to you, becomes flesh of your flesh, and cries out of chaos.

I leap up. God shouts and struggles in all this flesh.

Behind the stream of my mind and body, behind the stream of my race and all mankind, behind the stream of plants and animals, I watch with trembling the Invisible, treading on all visible things and ascending.

Behind his heavy and blood-spattered feet I hear all living things being trampled on and crushed.

His face is without laughter, dark and silent, beyond joy and sorrow, beyond hope.

I tremble. Are YOU my God? Your body is steeped in memory. Like one locked up in dungeons for many years, you have adorned your arms and chest with strange trees and hairy dragons, with gory adventures, with cries and chronologies.

Lord, my Lord, you growl like a wild beast! Your feet are covered with blood and mire, your hands are covered with blood and mire, your jaws are heavy millstones that grind slowly.

You clutch at trees and animals, you tread on man, you shout. You climb up the endless black precipice of death, and you tremble.

Where are you going? Pain increases, the light and the darkness increase. You weep, you hook onto me, you feed on my blood, you grow huge and strong, and then you kick at my heart.

Trees shout, animals and stars: "We are doomed!" Every living creature flings two huge hands as high as the heavens to seek help.

With his knees doubled up under his chin, with his hands spread toward the light, with the soles of his feet turned toward his back, God huddles in a knot in every cell of flesh.

When I break a fruit open, this is how every seed is revealed to me. When I speak to men, this what I discern in their thick and muddy brains.

God struggles in every thing, his hands flung upward toward the light. What light? Beyond and above every thing!

Pain is not the only essence of our God, nor is hope in a future life or a life on this earth, neither joy nor victory. Every religion that holds up to worship one of these primordial aspects of God narrows our hearts and our minds.

The essence of our God is STRUGGLE. Pain, joy, and hope unfold and labor within this struggle, world without end.

It is this ascension, the battle with the descending countercurrent, which gives birth to pain. But pain is not the absolute monarch. Every victory, every momentary balance on the ascent fills with joy every living thing that breathes, grows, loves, and gives birth.

But from every joy and pain a hope leaps out eternally to escape this pain and to widen joy.

And again the ascent begins—which is pain—and joy is reborn and new hope springs up once more. The circle never closes. It is not a circle, but a spiral which ascends eternally, ever widening, enfolding and unfolding the triune struggle.

What is the purpose of this struggle? This is what the wretched self-seeking mind of man is always asking, forgetting that the Great Spirit does not toil within the bounds of human time, place, or casualty.

The Great Spirit is superior to these human questionings. It teems with many rich and wandering drives which to our shallow minds seem contradictory; but in the essence of divinity they fraternize and struggle together, faithful comrades-in-arms.

The primordial Spirit branches out, overflows, struggles, fails, succeeds, trains itself. It is the Rose of the Winds.

Whether we want to or not, we also sail on and voyage, consciously or unconsciously, amid divine endeavors.

188

Indeed, even our march has eternal elements, without beginning or end, assisting God and sharing His perils.

God laughs, wails, kills, sets us on fire, and then leaves us in the middle of the way, charred embers.

And I rejoice to feel between my temples, in the flicker of an eyelid, the beginning and the end of the world.

I condense into a lightning moment the seeding, sprouting, blossoming, fructifying, and the disappearance of every tree, animal, man, star, and god.

All Earth is a seed planted in the coils of my mind. Whatever struggles for numberless years to unfold and fructify in the dark womb of matter bursts in my head like a small and silent lightning flash.

Ah! let us gaze intently on this lightning flash, let us hold it for a moment, let us arrange it into human speech.

Let us transfix this momentary eternity which encloses everything, past and future, but without losing in the immobility of language any of its gigantic erotic whirling.

You shall never be able to establish in words that you live in ecstasy. But struggle unceasingly to establish it in words. Battle with myths, with comparisons, with allegories, with rare and common words, with exclamations and rhymes, to embody it in flesh, to transfix it!

God, the Great Ecstatic, works in the same way. He speaks and struggles to speak in every way he can, with seas and with fires, with colors, with wings, with horns, with claws, with constellations and butterflies, that he may establish his ecstasy.

Like every other living thing, I also am in the center of the Cosmic whirlpool. I am the eye of monstrous rivers where everything dances about me as the circle continually narrows with greater vehemence till the heavens and earth plunge into the red pit of my heart.

33

*A*I-HA, BELOVED FRIEND:

Do you remember the verses of our old poet Wang Ai-hi that we sang so often in the moonlight?

Midnight.
Everyone is asleep in the house,
Even the water-clock has stopped.
But I cannot sleep, for the tenderly swaying flowers of spring
Whose shadow the moon casts on the wall
Are so beautiful that man cannot endure them.

Yes, I too hear that cry of the poet this year, Ai-Ha, my cousin! This spring is so gentle that I cannot sleep; I cannot contain my tears, Ai-Ha.

If I went out into the courtyard this evening dressed in my white gown and danced in the moonlight, I would be a little comforted, perhaps. But I would be ashamed. What if my father saw me from his window? What if a servant surprised me?

It would be better to cry out. To creep down our old creaking stairs, furtively open the door, run out into the street and hurry along the walls to the temple we loved so, Ai-Ha, when we were little and free—the Temple of Heaven!

Oh, how beautiful it must look this evening, in the moonlight! To climb the broad marble stairs, to cross the first terrace, then the second, then the third, with their great gates spread wide to the moon—and then, on the altar of the highest terrace, quite close to heaven, where our emperors offered the spring sacrifice, to stand alone, hands raised, to utter a cry!

That cry, perhaps, might have comforted my heart. For this spring, Ai-Ha, is too oppressive, it crushes me. Oh, in the good old times, remember how the girls our age had found the right path—the sunny path of consolation!

You know how willingly I have devoted myself to an austere and demanding task, one which is perhaps beyond my strength, which is perhaps unsuited to such poor creatures as women. But enough of that. I am awake, I am working, I help my brother. I have noticed that such labor is not too hard in autumn or in winter, but in spring, Ai-Ha, when the flowers open and the earth smells so sweet, it is suffocating!

My brother and I discuss the reports to be written on political or cultural questions; but my poor woman's lips tremble as they whisper the old spring songs.

If we too, my cousin, lived in those old times! How simple everything was then, and how beautiful! In the spring festivals we would have crossed the river wearing only a few orchid blossoms—we would have shivered at the contact of the living water, our breasts touched by the floating souls of the ancestors. And we would have stepped on the other bank happy and calm, like young brides. . . .

I see your lovely brows, my cousin, contract with distress. You take my hand, the way you used to do, and rest it gently on your heart. This gesture of yours has always moved me;

I never could resist it; I immediately confessed all my little secrets.

No, do not be distressed, beloved friend! No, I am not sad, I am very happy—but, you see, I can no longer express myself. By keeping silent so long, I have forgotten how to speak. And when at last I resolve to open my heart, my words leap and dance beyond my control instead of walking in good order. And I am ashamed. Speech, as our Sage says, should be exact and accurate, like the weights marked with the royal seal.

Yes, dear soul, I rest my hand on your heart and I say: Do not be distressed, I am not suffering. The spring is lovely, I am happy. Yes, I sleep very little, but such sleep is a precious substance, dense and sweet as honey. And my dreams are so beautiful that every night, toward dawn, as I slip into my bed, I quiver with impatience; I wait for dreams as the bride waits, with her ear pressed to the ground, for the joyous bells of her beloved's carriage.

One night I dreamed of a long, long journey: a white boat, the blue sea, the breeze blowing and stars rising on the horizon. I was lying on the prow and a man, sitting beside me, was telling me of distant lands, of white men with blue eyes, of young girls who run over the snow with their friends, laughing because they are free, happy and strong.

A great stork soared above us, holding some dry weeds in its bill. Was it building its nest?

Suddenly everything vanished and I found myself buried in the sand, my lips painted, my breast bare, like the figurehead of a shipwrecked vessel. The breeze blew through my hair, the stork had built its nest in my arms, and I felt drunk with happiness.

Yesterday, during the night of the full moon, I had another strange dream: I was at the bottom of a well filled with moonlight. I was happy—happy as a bee in the heart of some white lily. I was holding a book open on my knees; it was not Confucius, nor Lao-tse, nor any of our old poets.

I could not read by the moonlight, but the characters were

in relief, as in books for the blind. I stroked them with my fingertips, and slowly, endlessly caressing them, I spelled out a strange phrase and I trembled with happiness.

"Siu-lan, would you like us to make our way together toward this jade nothingness?"

I tipped my head back toward the moon, and I saw the letters of this sentence descend upon me in a dancing row, like a flock of swallows returning to find their nests in the spring.

You know how to interpret dreams; grandmother initiated you into that occult art. Dear friend, could you give me the key to these dreams? Could you explain why I trembled with happiness?

Yesterday I went to see the palaces of the Forbidden City. A gentle shower moistened my face. I was happy; no one could see that these drops streaming over my cheeks were not from the rain. For the first time, I wept as I walked over that ruin of greatness and pleasure.

I was not weeping for the dead emperors, nor for the great painted ladies who had died in this enormous gynaeceum haunted now by their ghosts, nor for the gods strangled by the ivy, without hands or feet now, their skin like that of miserable lepers.

No, no, cousin, I was weeping for something deeper, a humble, warm and troubling thing, like the heart of a young girl. . . .

And that evening, coming home, I locked myself in my huge empty room and I began to compose—don't laugh, Ai-Ha—a little poem.

I wrote it in red ink on my ivory tablets. I no longer remember these verses—there was a girl's heart in them, and the rain, and the faint cry of a wounded animal.

I hung the tablets outside my window, the spring rain fell during the night, and in the morning I found my tablets empty. Only the white wall was stained with red, like blood.

As you see, dear cousin, I am happy; I am playing, writing

verses, and offering them to the rain. To whom else could I offer them? I offer them to the rain and I think of you; I set my hand on my heart and I reveal my secret to you.

May this spring, dear soul, end well! May it bear all its fruits! May it take pity on me, and on you, and on all the young girls in the world!

SIU-LAN

34

*T*ODAY I RECEIVED the first letter from my friend
Kuge. In my heart's restlessness, this letter overflowing with faith and youth comforted me. I was ashamed
of my insignificant adventure and of the inertia in which
contemplation had plunged me.

These games of the tongue, these trains of thought had
fascinated me until I forgot our most urgent duty on earth—
action. To act, to mold, to penetrate. To embrace matter
as one embraces a woman. To make events as one makes
children. To enlist in the cause of the Universe, and do battle.

I read and reread Kuge's letter.

Tokyo, May 5

O White Demon from the Ocean!

Today we "little Japanese" celebrate the children's festival.
Giant carp of red cloth with black scales float in the wind,
for, as you know, the carp is our emblem of childhood. The

carp rises when the other fish, incapable of withstanding the current, submit and sink down.

Today, the finest room in the house is devoted to the young boy. On an improvised altar stands a little bronze or wooden samurai dressed in armor; the boy bows respectfully before this warrior-ancestor and swears to resemble him some day. To become a "samurai" in his heart, a fearless knight always ready to die—that is the greatest ambition of every Japanese boy.

On this holiday, the boy receives fine books on the exploits of the ancestors or on the great mission of Japan. If you open these books, white lords, you would immediately close them again with a sneer; in them you would find only arbitrary affirmations and narrow watchwords.

In the first pages, we often find this proud dialogue between the officer and the young conscript:

"Who is your leader?"

"The emperor."

"What is your duty?"

"To obey and sacrifice myself."

"What is 'great courage'?"

"Never to heed the enemy's number, but to advance."

"What is 'petty courage'?"

"To grow angry easily and use violence."

"What remains after man's death?"

"Glory."

God, country, emperor, that is our Trinity, more real, more profound than yours. Today, it is only in Germany, in Soviet Russia and in Italy that we can find such heroic discipline, such joyous submission of the individual to a high and dangerous goal. Other nations wallow in hypocrisy, pacifism, parliamentarianism and old-fashioned sentimentality. They have not understood that we have entered a new iron age.

So much the better. Let us advance before they realize it. Let us cultivate the virtues appropriate to this iron age: sacrifice, obedience, sobriety, severity, the joyous acceptance of death. After victory, in a few centuries, the other, feminine

196

virtues may flourish: kindness, sensibility, delicacy, tolerance. We have no time for them now!

Now let us sing the lines that Take Hirose, the hero of Port Arthur, composed in the midst of battle:

> *Infinite as the dome of heaven above us*
> *Is what we owe the Emperor.*
> *Enormous as the deep sea beneath us*
> *Is what we owe our country.*
> *Now is the time to pay our debt!*

I am returning with my schoolboys from a pilgrimage to the house of General Noghi. He is one of our great examples of a warrior's life and death, and today I was to discuss him with the children.

We contemplated the little bare room where he committed hara-kiri in 1912, when our great emperor Meiji was being buried. He killed himself, on this matting, with his wife. Beside them were found these heroic and tender verses, composed by Noghi:

> *He is going to join the gods on high,*
> *My great lord.*
> *And I, my heart leaping, follow him in the sky.*

I felt moved myself; I gathered my schoolboys around me and began speaking vehemently:

"Love sports, exercise your bodies, breathe deeply, run, swim and fight, do not be afraid! Let the white men no longer mock us and call us dwarfs!

"Sharpen your minds, open your eyes! Study machines, airplanes, warships, cannons and factories! Never forget, engrave upon your minds this very simple thing: 'If we do not become superior to the white men, we are lost!'

"Hearts high, think of the ancestors! How can we follow their greatest desires most faithfully? By exceeding them. Only he who exceeds them truly follows the traditions of the great ancestors.

197

"Silence, discipline, persistence! Asia feeds 1,200 million souls, Europe only 400 million. We are the brain of Asia, we have a great responsibility. Work in silence and without cease. Our hour has come, my children!

"Which of you knows by heart the verses of the great samurai Katsu Kaissu?"

All the schoolboys raised their hands, shouting: "Me! Me! Me!"

"Then we can sing them together!"

And before the door of General Noghi, we began singing:

Smile before others, before yourself be severe.
In misfortune, remain intrepid, in daily life, cheerful;
When you are praised, remain impassive;
When you are derided, immobile!

I was inspired with enthusiasm. I exclaimed to my students: "Open your notebooks and write!"

Each boy took his little notebook out of his pocket and I began dictating our Decalogue:

1. Above all things, honor and duty.
2. Obey the emperor blindly.
3. Despise death; be ready to die at any moment.

Each time you leave your house, it must be as if you were never to return.

4. Harden your body and soul without pity.
5. Be polite to your friends.
6. Take cruel revenge upon your enemies.
7. Do not cry out or weep: stand fast!

"Now write in large characters these verses of our great Emperor Meiji: *Whether your position is high or low, expend yourself completely—that is your duty.*

And, White Man, you may laugh or smile as you wish. But at that moment, I felt my powers increase tenfold. I was

198

truly more grave, more intelligent, readier to live or die than I had ever been. Is this new energy an illusion? Blessed be illusion! By reacting against reality with an irresistible force, it becomes real.

In a powerful race, the great ancestors are the true fathers. In a powerful race, the spirits of the heroes enter the houses at night and sleep with the women. The other fathers, the living ones, procreate bodies; the ancestors plant souls in them.

A hard and austere life, a terrible effort in order to create a new kind of Japanese soul! *Fudoshin! Fudoshin!* The great Japanese virtue! The motionless rock, our heart!

Dear friend, once the festival of children was over, I returned to my home still seething; this daily contact with the children constantly rejuvenates me. Trying to make these boys into grown men I make myself into a child before their young bodies, their eager eyes.

Now I am alone in this modest little house that you know. I am taking my tea, and I think of you; your absence is more disagreeable to me than your presence. Do not laugh. For that is the greatest confession of friendship I can make to a white man.

I think of you and envy you: you are treading the sacred soil of our Mother China! Greet her three times, humbly, for me.

China is the motionless center of the earth. She alone can save Japan. Japan alone can save China. Together the two can save this degenerate world.

If in the great war that is coming Japan should be conquered, all the East will be covered with darkness. Why? Because no Western nation possesses true justice and love. But if Japan wins, China will be freed, India will be reborn, the whole world will be rid of Western materialism.

The day China and Japan join hands, a new era will begin for the world—a more human culture.

You white men will soon be crushed under your machines, rotting in the endless swamp of your materialism. You have lost the essence of man: the impulse toward something that is more than yourselves. It is just that you should vanish from the earth! For what is man if he is not tormented by the thought of the superhuman? A machine for producing excrement, nothing more.

The lot of renewing the world falls once more to us. "Each time virtue diminishes and vice prevails, I descend to aid humanity," Buddha says. Among you virtue has vanished; evil—lies, greed, hypocrisy, sensuality—prevails.

The new Krishna will descend upon the earth. Do not be distressed, dear white friend, if this time he has a yellow skin.

Kuge Nakaoka

I showed this enthusiastic letter to Li-Te.

"You see how they love China!" I said.

Li-Te glanced at the letter, his lips clamped. From time to time he moaned faintly and clenched his fists.

He handed back the letter: "Yes . . . yes," he muttered. "They love China—like a rice cake." He laughed sardonically. "But they won't get their filthy teeth into her." And he added in a murmur, "Ridiculous Don Quixotes!"

"Old Don Quixote," I answered, "may have been a little absurd: he had a tragic ideal that he tried to achieve by comic means. The Japanese have Quixotic ambitions, but the means they are using to achieve them are of an extreme perfection and modernism. Their method is patient, silent and sure."

Li-Te gnashed his teeth. I saw the effort he was making to contain his fury; his throat was filled with cries and insults. But he did not let them get past the wall of his clenched teeth. Finally he opened his mouth; he had turned very pale.

"Come to my room tonight!" he said. "I have something to tell you."

35

LEFT ALONE, I withdrew into myself and listened. Simple and stern words rose within me, decisive orders. The face of the Unknown grew more and more human and pale before me. A samurai emerged from my entrails, intransigent and desperate, armed in steel. . . .

The Cry within me gradually took the form of human words.

THE ACTION

The ultimate most holy form of theory is action.

Not to look on passively while the spark leaps from generation to generation, but to leap and to burn with it!

Action is the widest gate of deliverance. It alone can answer the questionings of the heart. Amid the labyrinthine complexities of the mind it finds the shortest route. No, it does not "find"—it creates its way, hewing to right and left through resistances of logic and matter.

Why did you struggle behind phenomena to track down the Invisible? What was the purpose of all your warlike, your erotic march through flesh, race, man, plants, and animals? Why the mystic marriage beyond these labors, the perfect embracement, the bacchic and raging contact in darkness and in light?

That you might reach the point from which you began—the ephemeral, palpitating, mysterious point of your existence—with new eyes, with new ears, with a new sense of taste, smell, touch, with new brains.

Our profound human duty is not to interpret or to cast light on the rhythm of God's march, but to adjust, as much as we can, the rhythm of our small and fleeting life to his.

Only thus may we mortals succeed in achieving something immortal, because then we collaborate with One who is Deathless.

Only thus may we conquer mortal sin, the concentration on details, the narrowness of our brains; only thus may we transubstantiate into freedom the slavery of earthen matter given us to mold.

Amid all these things, beyond all these things every man and nation, every plant and animal, every god and demon charges upward like an army inflamed by an incomprehensible, unconquerable Spirit.

We struggle to make this Spirit visible, to give it a face, to encase it in words, in allegories and thoughts and incantations, that it may not escape us.

But it cannot be contained in the twenty-six letters of an alphabet which we string out in rows; we know that all these words, these allegories, these thoughts, and these incantations are, once more, but a new mask with which to conceal the Abyss.

Yet only in this manner, by confining immensity, may we labor within the newly incised circle of humanity.

What do we mean by "labor"? To fill up this circle

with desires, with anxieties, and with deeds; to spread out and reach frontiers until, no longer able to contain us, they crack and collapse. By thus working with appearances, we widen and increase the essence.

For this reason our return to appearances, after our contact with essence, possesses an incalculable worth.

We have seen the highest circle of spiraling powers. We have named this circle God. We might have given it any other name we wished: Abyss, Mystery, Absolute Darkness, Absolute Light, Matter, Spirit, Ultimate Hope, Ultimate Despair, Silence.

But we have named it God because only this name, for primordial reasons, can stir our hearts profoundly. And this deeply felt emotion is indispensable if we are to touch, body with body, the dread essence beyond logic.

Within this gigantic circle of divinity we are in duty bound to separate and perceive clearly the small, burning arc of our epoch.

On this barely perceptible flaming curve, feeling the onrush of the entire circle profoundly and mystically, we travel in harmony with the Universe, we gain impetus and dash into battle.

Thus, by consciously following the onrush of the Universe, our ephemeral action does not die with us.

It does not become lost in a mystical and passive contemplation of the entire circle; it does not scorn holy, humble, and daily necessity.

Within its narrow and blood-drenched ditch it stoops and labors steadfastly, conquering easily both space and time within a small point of space and time—for this point follows the divine onrush of the entire circle.

I do not care what face other ages and other people have given to the enormous, faceless essence. They have crammed it with human virtues, with rewards and punishments, with certainties. They have given a face to their hopes and fears, they have submitted their anarchy to a rhythm, they have found a higher justification by which to live and labor. They have fulfilled their duty.

But today we have gone beyond these needs; we have shattered this particular mask of the Abyss; our God no longer fits under the old features.

Our hearts have overbrimmed with new agonies, with new luster and silence. The mystery has grown savage, and God has grown greater. The dark powers ascend, for they have also grown greater, and the entire human island quakes.

Let us stoop down to our hearts and confront the Abyss valiantly. Let us try to mold once more, with our flesh and blood, the new, contemporary face of God.

For our God is not an abstract thought, a logical necessity, a high and harmonious structure made of deductions and speculations.

He is not an immaculate, neutral, odorless, distilled product of our brains, neither male nor female.

He is both man and woman, mortal and immortal, dung and spirit. He gives birth, fecundates, slaughters—death and Eros in one—and then he begets and slays once more, dancing spaciously beyond the boundaries of a logic which cannot contain the antinomies.

My God is not Almighty. He struggles, for he is in peril every moment; he trembles and stumbles in every living thing, and he cries out. He is defeated incessantly, but rises again, full of blood and earth, to throw himself into battle once more.

He is full of wounds, his eyes are filled with fear and stubbornness, his jawbones and temples are splintered. But he does not surrender, he ascends; he ascends with his feet, with his hands, biting his lips, undaunted.

My God is not All-holy. He is full of cruelty and savage justice, and he chooses the best mercilessly. He is without compassion; he does not trouble himself about men or animals; nor does he care for virtues and ideas. He loves *all these things for a moment, then smashes them eternally and passes on.*

He is a power that contains all things, that begets all things. He begets them, loves them, and destroys them. And if we say, "Our God is an erotic wind and shatters all bodies that he may drive on," and if we remember that Eros always works through blood and tears, destroying every individual without mercy—then we shall approach his dread face a little closer.

My God is not All-knowing. His brain is a tangled skein of light and darkness which he strives to unravel in the labyrinth of the flesh.

He stumbles and fumbles. He gropes to the right and turns back; swings to the left and sniffs the air. He struggles above chaos in anguish. Crawling, straining, groping for unnumbered centuries, he feels the muddy coils of his brain being slowly suffused with light.

On the surface of his heavy, pitch-black head he begins with an indescribable struggle to create eyes by which to see, ears by which to hear.

My God struggles on without certainty. Will he conquer? Will he be conquered? Nothing in the Universe is certain. He flings himself into uncertainty; he gambles all his destiny at every moment.

He clings to warm bodies; he has no other bulwark. He shouts for help; he proclaims a mobilization throughout the Universe.

It is our duty, on hearing his Cry, to run under his flag, to fight by his side, to be lost or to be saved with him.

God is imperiled. He is not almighty, that we may cross our hands, waiting for certain victory. He is not all-holy, that we may wait trustingly for him to pity and to save us.

Within the province of our ephemeral flesh all of God is imperiled. He cannot be saved unless we save him with our own struggles; nor can we be saved unless he is saved.

We are one. From the blind worm in the depths of

the ocean to the endless arena of the Galaxy, only one person struggles and is imperiled: You. And within your small and earthen breast only one thing struggles and is imperiled: the Universe.

We must understand well that we do not proceed from a unity of God to the same unity of God again. We do not proceed from one chaos to another chaos, neither from one light to another light, nor from one darkness to another darkness. What would be the value of our life then? What would be the value of all life?

But we set out from an almighty chaos, from a thick abyss of light and darkness tangled. And we struggle—plants, animals, men, ideas—in this momentary passage of individual life, to put in order the Chaos within us, to cleanse the abyss, to work upon as much darkness as we can within our bodies and to transmute it into light.

We do not struggle for ourselves, nor for our race, not even for humanity.

We do not struggle for Earth, nor for ideas. All these are the precious yet provisional stairs of our ascending God, and they crumble away as soon as he steps upon them in his ascent.

In the smallest lightning flash of our lives, we feel all of God treading upon us, and suddenly we understand: if we all desire it intensely, if we organize all the visible and invisible powers of earth and fling them upward, if we all battle together like fellow combatants eternally vigilant—then the Universe might possibly be saved.

It is not God who will save us—it is we who will save God, by battling, by creating, and by transmuting matter into spirit.

But all our struggle may go lost. If we tire, if we grow faint of spirit, if we fall into panic, then the entire Universe becomes imperiled.

Life is a crusade in the service of God. Whether we wished to or not, we set out as crusaders to free—not the

206

Holy Sepulchre—but that God buried in matter and in our souls.

Every body, every soul is a Holy Sepulchre. Every seed of grain is a Holy Sepulchre; let us free it! The brain is a Holy Sepulchre; God sprawls within it and battles with death; let us run to his assistance!

God gives the signal for battle, and I, too, rush to the attack, trembling.

Whether I straggle behind as a deserter or battle valiantly, I know that I shall always fall in battle. But on the first occasion my death would be sterile, for with the destruction of my body my soul would also be lost and scattered to the winds.

On the second occasion, I would descend into earth like a fruit brimming with seed. Though my breath abandon my body to rot, it would organize new bodies and continue the battle.

My prayer is not the whimpering of a beggar nor a confession of love. Nor is it the trivial reckoning of a small tradesman: Give me and I shall give you.

My prayer is the report of a soldier to his general: This is what I did today, this is how I fought to save the entire battle in my own sector, these are the obstacles I found, this is how I plan to fight tomorrow.

My God and I are horsemen galloping in the burning sun or under drizzling rain. Pale, starving, but unsubdued, we ride and converse.

"Leader!" I cry. He turns his face toward me, and I shudder to confront his anguish.

Our love for each other is rough and ready, we sit at the same table, we drink the same wine in this low tavern of life.

As we clink our glasses, swords clash and resound, loves and hates spring up. We get drunk, visions of slaughter ascend before our eyes, cities crumble and fall in our brains, and though we are both wounded and screaming with pain, we plunder a huge Palace.

36

*T*HE MOON was rising, enormous and livid, with slits for eyes.

I leaned toward the coolie who had pulled me in his ricksha. He stopped in front of a gate garlanded with red lanterns. He was covered with sweat. His cheeks were hollow, his eyes dim; opium had wasted his flesh, shriveled his bones. What little soul he had left shivered in his body like an old baboon.

"Why do you smoke?"

He stared at me with his cloudy, lashless, red-rimmed eyes: "My lord, life is hard," he whined.

Yes, life is hard, he had to smoke. Opium—religion, art, love, glory, ideas—is the only gateway to salvation.

This filthy coolie forgets his vermin and his hunger, smoking the miraculous drug. Others smoke God, an idea, or a woman. The coolie, dressed in silk, slowly enters paradise, borne by the sweet, bluish smoke. Climbing into this immaterial ricksha, he rides over reality like the gods of the beautiful Chinese woodcuts who sail, legs crossed, over white puffs of cloud.

A heartless power, a dragon with steel scales has forged these crushing fetters of reality; they are heavy, unjust and lice-ridden. But man raises a second level of existence above this cruel world. The opium smoke fulfills and perfects the work of God. Life, like a placid hen, is transformed into a peacock and spreads its tail.

The soul's value is judged only by the quality of the opium it absorbs. Woe to the soul that does not smoke!

This coolie is my brother in opium. I smile at him. "Yes," I say, clapping him on the shoulder without repugnance. "Yes, life is hard; we'll both smoke!"

The night was creeping over the roofs like a black panther. A few big stars hung in a chain around its neck.

I felt mortally sad. The human soul is a miracle, a spring that leaps out of the mud of the flesh, ignorant of where it is going and what it desires and why it has this incomprehensible and unnatural mania for rising—for rising and suffering.

All day long, I had scarcely once seen Siu-lan. For a moment I had glimpsed her leaning by her window, very pale, very sad. A woman's heart is a wound that never heals; if you touch it, even with a peacock feather, it shrieks in pain.

I went up to Li-Te's room this evening: a bare, ascetic, cold place. There was only one enormous painting on the wall: "The Great Wall of China." It rose and sank, crossing the mountains, fierce and indomitable, sinuous as a dragon.

"The worker who leaves a fissure in the masonry into which a nail might be driven will be condemned to death." This was the order of the great emperor Shih Huang Ti who built it. The spotless purity, the thirst for an absolute, the inexpugnable fortress—thus should we build our lives.

But Li-Te's strident voice interrupted my reflections. "Dear friend," he exclaimed triumphantly, "I have some good news for you. Are you ready to hear it?"

"I am always ready for good news," I answered, though I could not manage to check my anxiety.

Li-Te's eyes looked fierce, flashing with yellow glints.

"We have her at last!" he said in a low voice, and came closer to me in order to enjoy my surprise. I heard his panting breath. And as my eyes questioned him, he continued:

"She escaped us four times. Four times in ten years. But now it's over. She's fallen into our trap."

"But who are you talking about?" I exclaimed. "I don't understand!"

"She was bringing money to her allies—the Chinese traitors!" Li-Te went on, carried away by a hideous gaiety. "We caught her in the act; she won't get out of it this time. . . . My condolences, dear friend!"

He held out his hand with a laugh.

"But for the love of God," I exclaimed, "who are you talking about?"

"About your friend. About Joshiro!"

"Li-Te," I exclaimed, "didn't you take pity on her?"

"Pity?" he roared. "Me? Take pity on her?"

"She loves you . . ." I said.

He looked hard into my eyes; his voice deepened. "Aren't you ashamed?" he cried. "Why do you mix up these individual miseries with the great struggle?"

I fell silent, abashed. I left the cruel house.

To see naked women, to drink alcohol, to smoke opium. To forget. To forget Joshiro, the captive panther. To forget Siu-lan, with her omnipotent and silent lips. To enter, this night, into other forms of matter—to break the fetters that bound me. . . .

The sky was pure and silent; over the earth, lascivious cries, laughter, and the rustle of silk robes. The cabarets are opening, their dragon gates huge and wide as those of hell. The hour is propitious: the Chinese courtesans make their great entrances: supple, slender, flat-chested, hipless, straight and severe as swords. Scabbards of blue, black or scarlet silk, slit up to the thigh. They walk quickly; at each step, the naked, lacquered body is revealed, gleaming like steel armor.

And above this dangerous body rises the startling mask: a flat face, like that of some enraged cobra. The slanting eyes, motionless and cold, allure you and you fling yourself into them, dizzy.

A skinny, wretchedly dressed young Chinese in a student's cap was watching from the doorstep of the café. The shudders were almost invisible on his wizened skin. He watched the women walking in, leaving a wisp of musk in the warm night air; he watched the white men, freshly bathed, pomaded, excited at being able to satisfy, at last, all the ignominies they nursed in secret.

The poor student stared greedily at everything. I took pity on this young body panting on the threshold of happiness.

"Good evening, young man," I said. "If you like, let us go in together; I'll buy you a drink . . . and a woman, if that is what your heart desires."

He turned and stared at me in silence. His lips parted; he began to laugh hideously, like a death's head.

"Do you understand?"

"Yes, yes, I understand," he answered abruptly in a lisping English. "Liquor . . . women . . . You're a satiated bourgeois, aren't you?"

"And you're a Communist?"

"I'm a man suffering, that's all!" he said, and stared back into the lighted café.

People were dancing on the gleaming floor. All sexes. Men, women, effeminate boys, viragos, eunuchs . . . the blond English, the square-shouldered American pseudoathletes—all shouted together. The yellow vampires, male and female, sucked their blood.

"I'm suffering too," I answered.

The young man turned back; he looked at me again and tossed his head: "What from?"

What could I answer? To suffer from love seemed to me, at that moment, too pathetic a pain, too bourgeois a pastime. I was ashamed before this violent and poor young man who seemed to suffer from some infinitely nobler wound.

"You see!" he sneered. "You don't even know what from. Bad digestion?"

"Let's go inside," I said. "We can talk better there."

"No!" the young man said, stiffening.

"Then why have you come here?"

"To see . . . To feast my eyes . . . Then to go back to my room and—"

He hesitated, not finding the word.

"And weep?"

"Weep!" he exclaimed furiously.

"I understand," I said, touching his arm. "Don't fly into a rage, please. I understand now; this abominable spectacle whips up your virtues; it excites you to combat. You want to bring justice into the world . . ."

"What justice?" he demanded. "You must be an idealist, a bourgeois sentimentalist. *Justice!*"

How well I understood this tragic banter, these jeers that tore the heart! *Justice!* Yes, this yellow student was right. What justice?

A proud and wounded heart does not ask for justice. Justice is not enough; such a heart scorns justice. This wretched virtue is good for the herd, for the mendicant hearts that are content with a piece of bread, content to lick the fat hand that offers it to them.

"Justice!" the young student growled between his rotted teeth. "Justice! No, vengeance! A vengeance worse than their crime—terrible, beautiful and unjust!"

He turned toward me, shivering: "You understand?" He stared at me again, and again tossed his head. "No," he said, "you don't understand. Go on in! Join your brothers. Have a good time. And quickly!"

He pushed me inside and closed the door behind me, emitting his dreadful death's head laugh.

I walked over to a corner and sat down alone.

Yes, I understood this young Chinese with his rebellious heart; but I wanted to see, to hear, to absorb this spectacle that excites proud hearts and impels them to vengeance. To take part in these joys, which are dangerous only to weak and sentimental souls; to measure the value of my soul by driving it into danger. . . .

And Siu-lan? I asked. And Joshiro?

They were already far away, on the other shore.

Ambushed in my corner like a carrion crow waiting for my turn, I savored this spectacle that degraded my race.

"Eat, brutes, drink! Embrace your women, but quickly!" croaked the crow deep in my throat.

As the night advanced, the women grew excited and the men lost their souls. At dawn, every member of the white race would doubtless be rolling across the filthy floor, and the yellow women would be raising their heads, endlessly licking their lips.

A beautiful Chinese girl sitting beside me on the velvet banquette was smoking a tiny perfumed cigarette and staring at me without a smile.

I stretched out my hand to make sure she was real, that her flesh resisted touch, and that her smooth black hair was not a mere condensation of ether. And I was happy to discover that this body existed.

I felt my soul hesitate before the eternal path that forks at every step. My soul is full of unsatisfied curiosities, it is not resigned to depriving itself of any of earth's temptations; at the same time it is too proud to let itself be abased.

That night I called on the voluptuous and balanced genius of my race, which first succeeded in combining logic and intoxication into one tragic vision.

I gazed intently at the coupling of yellow and white. Concentrating without rage or pity on the wild beast within me—my totem—I cried: "Of the three paths, O my soul journeying among the sirens, of the three paths, O my soul!

"Either give yourself up utterly to the joys of earth, and rot, or abstain from all joy and die in sanctity. It is the third path—that of Ulysses the insatiable and cunning—that remains the best of all!"

37

$\mathcal{S}$HORTLY BEFORE dawn I returned to the house.
I opened the door in silence and walked around
the little screen that stands at the entrance of every Chinese
house to keep evil spirits from entering the courtyard. For
evil spirits—the glances of passers-by—move only in a straight
line.

I zigzagged through the courtyard, across the little flower
garden.

I stopped for a moment to inhale the perfume of spring.
Yes, life was so simple, happiness a fruit native to the earth.
The plant rooted in the soil, feeding on water, air, sun, per-
petual surge of sap and freely disciplined architecture—that
is the supreme model, the creature most faithful to the great
rhythm of the Universe.

Why have we abandoned the plant's way?

Why has life abondoned that sure form to join in the fate
of the animals, a fate so risky, so uncertain, bristling with
such dangers? Who, then, is the great proud and scatter-
brained Gambler suddenly staking his all?

Here in China the white man, the anxious and rapacious beast of prey, can at last recover the generous and just tone, the norm. Here the game of the great Unknown is more conservative and prudent. It is in harmony with earth, heaven and with death, recognizing its limits, filling the field of action with everyday virtue—neither advancing by leaps nor dancing like a drunkard but quite simply walking with firm and rhythmical strides. Behaving of course with dignity, but at the same time with grace. For how can one achieve supreme wisdom with furrowed brows?

Siu-lan will be my initiation—intense strength and pliant grace. She alone can bring a smile to my insatiable lips that until now could only laugh too loud or gnaw at themselves. . . .

The jade-colored moon was paling on the horizon; the morning star, like a great spark from some conflagration, leaped up in the east.

"I won't go to sleep," I decided. "The moment is too lovely; even the sweetest dream could never match it. I'll turn back to the street and surprise the city as it wakens."

But just as I was turning around, a shadow suddenly appeared at the other end of the little garden, already bathed in morning light.

I heard a clicking of bracelets and smelled a gentle perfume of clove.

"Siu-lan!"

Siu-lan was walking slowly between the trees; her face, her throat, her hands gleamed faintly in the blue-green light of dawn, then vanished again in the moving shadows of the leaves, almost as though she were dying and resuscitating at each moment.

I was so happy that I could not bear to disturb this ineffable moment by any sudden movement.

Oh, if time could stand still! To see that body of desire approaching for the rest of my life, approaching and never reaching me! To smell that redolent perfume of an unknown race!

But Siu-lan was already standing before me, smiling.

"Siu-lan," I murmured, "why?"

"I couldn't sleep," she answered. "Forgive me . . ."

Gently I took her hand: "Siu-lan, you're trembling . . ."

"I'm cold." She hid her hands deep in the sleeves of her gown.

A cock crowed in the courtyard; the little birds began chirping in the branches, timidly, feverishly—a lover's delirium. I felt within my breast the heart of the world filled with new leaves and glowworms.

Siu-lan looked up; her throat gleamed in the cool light.

"The lark," she murmured.

At this word my heart overflowed. "Siu-lan," I cried, "Siu-lan . . ." And I greedily took her face between my hands.

But as I was lowering my trembling lips, Siu-lan escaped with the agility of some wild creature. She bowed to the ground and humbly embraced my knees.

"Siu-lan, what are you doing?"

But she pressed my knees against her breasts in silence.

I felt my whole being dissolve with tenderness. A total, obedient, jubilant union, the happiness of the dancing young leaf firmly attached to its branch!

The lark, head thrown back, was singing deep in my heart. I felt the conspiracy of things subtly meshing around me: the morning hour, the singing bird, the half-loosened hair of this woman exhaling its age-old, warm and disturbing scent, and within me the mysterious traitor about to throw open the fortress. . . .

For a moment I restrained this ineffable shudder on the threshold of fulfillment. I do not know which delight is greater: to remain standing on joy's threshold and tell oneself: "If I wish, I enter; if I do not wish, I will not enter. I am free."

Or else, without losing a moment, to cross this threshold and enter. . . . I believe that shudder on the threshold is the supreme joy. . . .

Suddenly Siu-lan started. She stiffened, cocked her head, alarmed.

The inner door to the garden opened and on the threshold, enormous, white-gowned and frighteningly pale, appeared the old mandarin.

"My father!" Siu-lan whispered, motionless.

The old man stared at us with wide eyes; the heavy mass of his flesh moved. He took a step.

He seemed very tired; he stopped, sighing deeply, like a bull being slaughtered.

Then he took another step toward us. He stopped again, as if he could no longer move—as if the distance between his daughter and himself were immeasurable and he dared not attempt to cross it.

Siu-lan stood up; motionless, she stared at the old man who swayed in the soft light. I felt her trembling from head to foot.

"Siu-lan," I murmured, taking her hand.

I wanted to draw her to me, but she freed herself, taking pity on her father, and with a gasp took the few steps that separated her from him; she clasped her hands and bowed to him.

The old mandarin stretched his arm out over Siu-lan, as though he wanted to protect her.

The girl nestled against his chest, and the pair, arms around each other, slowly vanished into the house.

38

$\mathcal{I}$ WENT TO my room with a heavy heart. The first
sunbeams had already touched the walls of the
house, falling through the window on a tiny bouquet of
yellow flowers on a black lacquer table. I trembled when I
recognized them. Had not Siu-lan picked them one happy
evening in the garden of the jade Buddha?

"Siu-lan . . ." I murmured, and my head swam. Siu-lan,
her hard breasts pressed against my knees that melted with
longing . . .

I bit my lips to free myself of this terrible joy. I glanced
around the room that was so tenderly lit by the morning
sun. On the walls, the inscriptions awoke, black on yellow,
disturbing. Once again the mysterious jungle of Chinese
script stirred.

I stared one after the other at these inscriptions on the
silk banners, alarmed. Li-Te had translated them for me, in
his incisive voice.

The one over the door: "The barbarian has a tumultuous

soul; he is not master of himself. He disturbs the order of the Universe."

The one over my bed: "Man must achieve perfection in order to fulfill his own law." And the third, a single word, over my desk: "Tao."

I felt exasperated; all these austere voices were trying to impose an alien rhythm upon my nature, which is inspired only by revolt. What is the fulfillment of my own law? To disturb order, to violate convention, to turn from the path of the ancestors. To wander through the forbidden, in the proud and perilous regions of the uncertain. To receive without flinching—indeed, as a blessing—the curses of father and mother alike. To have the courage to be alone.

If only I could dissolve the torpor that benumbs Siu-lan's noble soul!

I saw her again in my mind's eye, pressed against her father's huge body, vanishing into the shadows. I felt defeated; she had hesitated a moment, but soon lowered her head and yielded to this huge mass of flesh.

I stretched out on the bed and closed my eyes. Gradually my heart grew calm.

Strident cries rang out within me, hisses, jeers, a mocking laughter. I leaped up from the bed.

All my pain vanished. It had assumed a meaning which infinitely exceeded my miserable being.

At the moment when I was voluptuously sinking—like a hog—into the filthy bog of the self where this tragic and laughable trifle (a man, a woman who love each other) threatened to make me happy, something cried out within me and I felt a whiplash.

To embrace, forget, sleep! Let the soul bloom in the calm and abundant flesh, like a plant that feeds on marsh water. . . .

But the mocking laughter rang out within me, and the whip cracked again.

At least, if I could enjoy the great vision! There is no peak so high and so steep, no delight so pure! What more could one desire?

I renounce the joys of the flesh, of oblivion and sleep. I seek only that heroic union with the Invisible made visible by the strength of desire.

O terrible mouth crying out within me, "*Help!*" I renounce Siu-lan to you; but let me have the utter joy of supreme contemplation. Beyond it, nothing else dares exist!

A sarcastic laugh exploded in my heart; a clear voice rose within me and moaned:

"God is not a pig, nor a philosopher, nor an ascetic. He is a Warrior who marches on. March with him! Leave behind you your small joys and your ridiculous virtues! That is good which leaps forward and runs to help God; that is evil which turns back and impedes the divine advance. Become good—that is, manly, unsatiated, pitiless!"

Flushed with shame, I listened to the voice:

We, as human beings, are all miserable persons, heartless, small, insignificant. But within us a superior essence drives us ruthlessly upward.

From within this human mire divine songs have welled up, great ideas, violent loves, an unsleeping assault full of mystery, without beginning or end, without purpose, beyond every purpose.

Humanity is such a lump of mud, each one of us is such a lump of mud. What is our duty? To struggle so that a small flower may blossom from the dunghill of our flesh and mind.

Out of things and flesh, out of hunger, out of fear, out of virtue and sin, struggle continually to create God.

How does the light of a star set out and plunge into black eternity in its immortal course? The star dies, but the light never dies; such also is the cry of freedom.

Out of the transient encounter of contrary forces which constitute your existence, strive to create whatever immortal thing a mortal may create in this world—a Cry.

And this Cry, abandoning to the earth the body which gave it birth, proceeds and labors eternally.

I surrendered myself to this rhythm, set aside my small erotic pain and allowed myself to be carried away toward the great Eros, the only thing worthy for a soul that esteems itself.

A vehement Eros runs through the Universe. It is like the ether: harder than steel, softer than air.

It cuts through and passes beyond all things, it flees and escapes. It does not repose in warm detail nor enslave itself in the beloved body. It is a Militant Eros. Behind the shoulders of its beloved it perceives mankind surging and roaring like waves, it perceives animals and plants uniting and dying, it perceives the Lord imperiled and shouting to it: "Save me!"

Eros? What other name may we give that impetus which becomes enchanted as soon as it casts its glance on matter and then longs to impress its features upon it? It confronts the body and longs to pass beyond it, to merge with the other erotic cry hidden in that body, to become one till both may vanish and become deathless by begetting sons.

It approaches the soul and wishes to merge with it inseparably so that "you" and "I" may no longer exist; it blows on the mass of mankind and wishes, by smashing the resistances of mind and body, to merge all breaths into one violent gale that may lift the earth!

Eros is the spirit, the breathing of God on earth.

It descends on men in whatever form it wishes—as dance, as love, as hunger, as religion, as slaughter. It does not ask our permission.

In these hours of crisis God struggles to knead flesh and brains together in the trough of earth, to cast all this mass of dough into the merciless whirlwind of his rotation and to give it a face—his face.

He does not choke with disgust, he does not despair in the dark, earthen entrails of men. He toils, proceeds, and devours the flesh; he clings to the belly, the heart, the mind and the phallos of man.

He is not the upright head of a family; he does not portion out either bread or brains equally to his children. Injustice, Cruelty, Longing, and Hunger are the four steeds that drive his chariot on this roughhewn earth of ours.

God is never created out of happiness or comfort or glory, but out of shame and hunger and tears.

At every moment of crisis an array of men risk their lives in the front ranks as standard-bearers of God to fight and take upon themselves the whole responsibility of the battle.

Once long ago it was the priests, the kings, the noblemen, or the burghers who created civilizations and set divinity free.

Today God is the common worker made savage by toil and rage and hunger. He stinks of smoke and wine and meat. He swears and hungers and begets children; he cannot sleep; he shouts and threatens in the cellars and garrets of earth.

The air has changed, and we breathe in deeply a spring laden and filled with seed. Cries rise up on every side. Who shouts? It is we who shout—the living, the dead, and the unborn. But at once we are crushed by fear, and we fall silent.

And then we forget—out of laziness, out of habit, out of cowardice. But suddenly the Cry tears at our entrails once more, like an eagle.

For the Cry is not outside us, it does not come from a great distance that we may escape it. It sits in the center of our hearts, and cries out.

God shouts: "Burn your houses! I am coming! Whoever has a house cannot receive me!

"Burn your ideas, smash your thoughts! Whoever has found the solution cannot find me.

"I love the hungry, the restless, the vagabonds. They

are the ones who brood eternally on hunger, on rebellion, on the endless road—on ME!

"I am coming! Leave your wives, your children, your ideas, and follow me. I am the great Vagabond.

"Follow! Stride over joy and sorrow, over peace and justice and virtue! Forward! Smash these idols, smash them all; they cannot contain me. Smash even yourself that I may pass."

Set fire! This is our great duty today amid such immoral and hopeless chaos.

War against the unbelievers! The unbelievers are the satisfied, the satiated, the sterile.

Our hate is uncompromising because it knows that it works for love better and more profoundly than any weakhearted kindness.

We hate, we are never content, we are unjust, we are cruel and filled with restlessness and faith; we seek the impossible, like lovers.

Sow fire to purify the earth! Let a more dreadful abyss open up between good and evil, let injustice increase, let Hunger descend to thresh our bowels, for we may not otherwise be saved.

We are living in a critical, violent moment of history; an entire world is crashing down, another has not yet been born. Our epoch is not a moment of equilibrium in which refinement, reconciliation, peace, and love might be fruitful virtues.

We live in a moment of dread assault, we stride over our enemies, we stride over our lagging friends, we are imperiled in the midst of chaos, we drown. We can no longer fit into old virtues and hopes, into old theories and actions.

The wind of devastation is blowing; this is the breath of our God today; let us be carried away in its tide! The wind of devastation is the first dancing surge of the creative rotation. It blows over every head and every city, it knocks down houses and ideas, it passes over desolate wastes, and it shouts: "Prepare yourselves! War! It's War!"

This is our epoch, good or bad, beautiful or ugly, rich or poor—we did not choose it. This is our epoch, the air we breathe, the mud given us, the bread, the fire, the spirit!

Let us accept Necessity courageously. It is our lot to have fallen on fighting times. Let us tighten our belts, let us arm our hearts, our minds, and our bodies. Let us take our place in battle!

War is the lawful sovereign of our age. Today the only complete and virtuous man is the warrior. For only he, faithful to the great pulse of our time, smashing, hating, desiring, follows the present command of our God.

The essence of our God is obscure. It ripens continuously; perhaps victory is strengthened with our every valorous deed, but perhaps even all these agonizing struggles toward deliverance and victory are inferior to the nature of divinity.

Whatever it might be, we fight on without certainty, and our virtue, uncertain of any rewards, acquires a profound nobility.

We do not see, we do not hear, we do not hate, we do not love as once we did. Earth takes on a new virginity. Bread and water and women take on a new flavor.

Everyone has his own particular road which leads him to liberation—one the road of virtue, another the road of evil.

If the road leading you to your liberation is that of disease, of lies, of dishonor, it is then your duty to plunge into disease, into lies, into dishonor, that you may conquer them. You may not otherwise be saved.

If the road which leads you to your liberation is the road of virtue, of joy, of truth, it is then your duty to plunge into virtue, into joy, into truth, that you may conquer them and leave them behind you. You may not otherwise be saved.

We do not fight our dark passions with a sober,

bloodless, neutral virtue which rises above passion, but with other, more violent passions.

We leave our door open to sin. We do not plug up our ears with wax that we may not listen to the Sirens. We do not bind ourselves, out of fear, to the mast of a great idea; nor by hearing and by embracing the Sirens do we abandon our ship, and perish.

On the contrary, we seize the Sirens and pitch them into our boat so that even they may voyage with us; and we continue on our way. This, my comrades, is our new Asceticism, our Spiritual Exercises!

God cries to my heart: "Save me!"

God cries to men, to animals, to plants, to matter: "Save me!"

Listen to your heart and follow him. Shatter your body and awake: We are all one.

Love man because you are he.

Love animals and plants because you were they, and now they follow you like faithful co-workers and slaves.

Love your body; only with it may you fight on this earth and turn matter into spirit.

Love matter. God clings to it tooth and nail, and fights. Fight with him.

Die every day. Be born every day. Deny everything you have every day. The superior virtue is not to be free but to fight for freedom.

39

$\mathcal{D}$O NOT CONDESCEND *to ask: "Shall we conquer? Shall we be conquered?" Fight on!*

So may the enterprise of the Universe, for an ephemeral moment, for as long as you are alive, become your own enterprise. This, Comrades, is our new Decalogue.

All this world, all this rich, endless flow of appearances is not a deception, a multicolored phantasmagoria of our mirroring mind. Nor is it absolute reality which lives and evolves freely, independent of our mind's power.

It is not the resplendent robe which arrays the mystic body of God. Nor the obscurely translucent partition between man and mystery.

All this world that we see, hear, and touch is that accessible to the human senses, a condensation of the two enormous powers of the Universe permeated with all of God.

One power descends and wants to scatter, to come

to a standstill, to die. The other power ascends and strives for freedom, for immortality.

These two armies, the dark and the light, the armies of life and of death, collide eternally. The visible signs of this collision are, for us, plants, animals, men.

The antithetical powers collide eternally; they meet, fight, conquer and are conquered, become reconciled for a brief moment, and then begin to battle again throughout the Universe—from the invisible whirlpool in a drop of water to the endless cataclysm of stars in the Galaxy.

Even the most humble insect and the most insignificant idea are the military encampments of God. Within them, all of God is arranged in fighting position for a critical battle.

Even in the most meaningless particle of earth and sky I hear God crying out: "Help me!"

Everything is an egg in which God's sperm labors without rest, ceaselessly. Innumerable forces within and without it range themselves to defend it.

With the light of the brain, with the flame of the heart, I besiege every cell where God is jailed, seeking, trying, hammering to open a gate in the fortress of matter, to create a gap through which God may issue in heroic attack.

Lie in ambush behind appearances, patiently, and strive to subject them to laws. Thus may you open up roads through chaos and help the spirit on its course.

Impose order, the order of your brain, on the flowing anarchy of the world. Incise your plan of battle clearly on the face of the abyss.

Contend with the powers of nature, force them to the yoke of superior purpose. Free that spirit which struggles within them and longs to mingle with that spirit which struggles within you.

When a man fighting with chaos subdues a series of appearances to the laws of his mind and strictly confines these laws within the boundaries of reason, then the world breathes, the voices are ranged in order, the future becomes clarified, and all the dark and endless quantities of numbers are freed by submitting to mystical quality.

With the help of our minds we compel matter to come with us. We divert the direction of descending powers, we alter the course of the current, we transform slavery into freedom.

We do not only free God by battling and subduing the visible world about us; we also create God.

"Open your eyes," God shouts; "I want to see! Prick up your ears, I want to hear! March in the front ranks: you are my head!"

A stone is saved if we lift it from the mire and build it into a house, or if we chisel the spirit upon it.

The seed is saved—what do we mean by "saved"? It frees the God within it by blossoming, by bearing fruit, by returning to earth once more. Let us help the seed to save itself.

Every man has his own circle composed of trees, animals, men, ideas, and he is in duty bound to save this circle. He, and no one else. If he does not save it, he cannot be saved.

These are the labors each man is given and is in duty bound to complete before he dies. He may not otherwise be saved. For his own soul is scattered and enslaved in these things about him, in trees, in animals, in men, in ideas, and it is his own soul he saves by completing these labors.

If you are a laborer, then till the earth, help it to bear fruit. The seeds in the earth cry out, and God cries out within the seeds. Set him free! A field awaits its deliverance at your hands, a machine awaits its soul. You may never be saved unless you save them.

If you are a warrior, be pitiless; compassion is not in the periphery of your duty. Kill the foe mercilessly. Hear how God cries out in the body of the enemy: "Kill this body, it obstructs me! Kill it that I may pass!"

If you are a man of learning, fight in the skull, kill ideas and create new ones. God hides in every idea as in every cell of flesh. Smash the idea, set him free! Give him another, a more spacious idea in which to dwell.

If you are a woman, then love. Choose austerely among all men the father of your children. It is not you who make the choice, but the indestructible, merciless, infinite, masculine God within you. Fulfill all your duty, so over-brimming with bitterness, love, and valor. Give up all your body, so filled with blood and milk.

Say: "This child, which I hold suckling at my breast, shall save God. Let me give him all my blood and milk."

Profound and incommensurable is the worth of this flowing world: God clings to it and ascends, God feeds upon it and increases.

My heart breaks open, my mind is flooded with light, and all at once this world's dread battlefield is revealed to me as an erotic arena.

Two violent contrary winds, one masculine and the other feminine, met and clashed at a crossroads. For a moment they counterbalanced each other, thickened, and became visible.

This crossroads is the Universe. This crossroads is my heart.

This dance of the gigantic erotic collision is transmitted from the darkest particle of matter to the most spacious thought.

The wife of my God is matter; they wrestle with each other, they laugh and weep, they cry out in the nuptial bed of flesh.

They spawn and are dismembered. They fill sea, land, and air with species of plants, animals, men, and spirits. This primordial pair embraces, is dismembered, and multiplies in every living creature.

All the concentrated agony of the Universe bursts

out in every living thing. God is imperiled in the sweet ecstasy and bitterness of flesh.

But he shakes himself free, he leaps out of brains and loins, then clings to new brains and new loins until the struggle for liberation again breaks out from the beginning.

For the first time on this earth, from within our hearts and our minds, God gazes on his own struggle.

Joy! Joy! I did not know that all this world is so much part of me, that we are all one army, that windflowers and stars struggle to right and left of me and do not know me; but I turn to them and hail them.

The Universe is warm, beloved, familiar, and it smells like my own body. It is Love and War both, a raging restlessness, persistence and uncertainty.

Uncertainty and terror. In a violent flash of lightning I discern on the highest peak of power the final, the most fearful pair embracing: Terror and Silence. And between them, a Flame.

When, toward noon, I left my room my head was throbbing. The weather was warm, the little garden hummed to itself like a stanza in a poem.

Li-Te had not yet come downstairs; he was still working, exalted. I had heard his footsteps over my bedroom all morning; he walked back and forth, anxious, nervous, almost skipping.

At the other end of the garden I saw Siu-lan. She was standing with her hands crossed on her breast, looking very pale. Her eyes seemed larger than ever and were staring blindly.

I greeted her from a distance by bowing in silence, but she did not notice. Her eyes were riveted on her brother's window on the floor above.

The old mandarin, enthroned in his armchair, was smoking in front of the gate. He was like those huge granite elephants that lie in the Chinese plain, surveying an enormous calm landscape. He seemed very calm, but with a greenish, corpselike pallor. When his eyes fell on me I felt an unbearable discomfort.

I took several steps toward Siu-lan. She was still motionless, and now I could see her distressed expression very clearly.

"Siu-lan . . ." I murmured, in order not to startle her. "Siu-lan!"

She turned and looked at me, as if she had not expected my presence in the house. But she quickly controlled herself and a sad smile flickered over her lips.

I started to take her hand, but the old mandarin stirred heavily in his chair and I refrained.

I stared at Siu-lan with the fatuity of a man contemplating a woman ravaged by love. "Siu-lan," I said with a smile, "why so sad?"

She glanced at me with alarm, her eyes severe, and her face glowed with a dark radiance.

"No, not love," I told myself, with a shudder. "That is not love."

"Bad news?" I murmured.

"Yes," she answered in a choked voice.

She choked on the words as they came from her lips. "Betrayed . . . Our generals corrupted . . . The Japanese army is advancing."

"When? How?" I exclaimed. "Siu-lan, tell me, I beg you!"

But Siu-lan shrugged nervously. She was trembling from head to foot.

"Your Joshiro," she snarled. She stifled a cry. Li-Te had approached on his tiger's silent feet and stood between Siu-lan and myself.

He was very pale; in a few hours, he had grown terribly drawn. He didn't look at me, but tenderly took Siu-lan's little hand in his own. "Siu-lan," he murmured, "forgive me, I have a great favor to ask of you."

Siu-lan bowed, trembling.

"There is an order to take to our friends. We can't trust it to just anyone. You're the only one we have confidence in. Will you accept this delicate mission?"

Siu-lan bowed again; I could hear her irregular breathing. The old father, at the other end of the garden, cocked his head. The two canaries in the cage over the door began to sing with a divine unconcern.

"Will you?" Li-Te asked again in a low voice.

"Yes," Siu-lan whispered.

"It's dangerous . . ." Li-Te insisted.

Then Siu-lan raised her eyes and a smile of terrible sadness trembled on her lips. "All the better!" she said, her tone suddenly resolute.

I felt my knees buckle. The world grew misty before my eyes. I saw my dream collapse. Siu-lan's perfume and warmth would never accompany me then, in this short, hard life of ours! Those dreamed-of evenings of calm and happiness, the profound pleasure of penetrating an alien race by penetrating a woman of that race, and the sons that would spring forth between these two bodies, yellow and white—all lost!

I felt a heavy tear run down my cheek. Furious, I crushed it between my fingers. "Have you no shame?" I asked myself with disgust. "Have you no shame?"

Li-Te turned toward me. His teeth gleamed. "Your Joshiro," he said, as if he were continuing the sentence Siu-lan had begun. "In a few days, your Joshiro will be thrown to the dogs! Siu-lan will take her death warrant!" His voice shook with rage. "Have you any message for her?" he added, with a hideous little laugh.

I started. I had never loved this ugly, cynical and cruel Japanese girl; but at that moment, I felt at one with her, for eternity.

"Yes," I said, accepting the challenge. "I have something to tell her."

"Confide it to Siu-lan, please," Li-Te said harshly. "Should I leave?"

232

"No," I answered, "you can hear it, dear friend!" And turning toward Siu-lan, who was standing motionless and very pale between us: "Siu-lan, tell Joshiro from me, please, that I was here when you received her death warrant. And that I have understood."

"Is that all?" Li-Te asked sarcastically.

"Li-Te, you're inhuman!" I exclaimed, unable to control my distress a moment longer. "This woman—you once loved her, she loved you, she still loves you!"

Li-Te frowned; he opened his mouth a second, but closed it at once and his teeth grated.

"Li-Te," I said again, filled with a vague hope. "Li-Te, won't you answer?"

"I have already answered," he said between his teeth.

"What is your answer?"

"Death!"

"Li-Te! Li-Te!"

"Death!"

"But why? What was her crime?"

"She has debauched our generals, she has given herself to them all. In the morning, she gives them money. We caught her too late—they've already left the roads open and the Japanese are advancing. Do you understand? Tell me, do you understand? *Death!*"

The man with the scar appeared. Li-Te turned toward his sister: "Siu-lan," he said, "here is your guide. You will leave tomorrow. Wang," he said to the Chinese, "come with me!"

Li-Te walked quickly into the house. I followed him, appalled. Death! Yes, he's right . . . death! He is a warrior; his duty is to kill. Joshiro too was a warrior; what was her duty? To give her strong, thin body to the enemy generals, to suck their strength. To open the roads. To send the Japanese army toward the heart of China, Peking. To trample Li-Te's heart under her tiny feet.

Li-Te went up to his room followed by the silent Chinese. The old father had moved into the little sitting room, and his large eyes followed us with unconcern. There was something strangely calm and distant in his eyes this tragic day, something so detached that they reminded me of the immortal and empty eyes of statues.

Siu-lan came into the sitting room; she knelt before her father and poured his tea. The old man laid his heavy hand on Siu-lan's head and briefly caressed her beautiful black hair. He closed his eyes.

"Thank you," he murmured.

Siu-lan bowed to me and filled my tiny cup. She raised her eyes and looked at me for a long moment. There was no anger in her eyes now, but a calm, heroic grief.

"Siu-lan," I murmured, with an effort, "Siu-lan, are you leaving?"

"Yes," she answered, "leaving . . ."

I sat stunned; for the first time, in Siu-lan's eyes, I distinguished the same light I had discovered that first day in her brother's eyes.

"And what about me?" I murmured plaintively, like a child being abandoned. "Aren't you even giving me a thought, Siu-lan?"

"I have no time!" Siu-lan answered, almost shouting.

"No time?"

She clenched her lips, beyond words. She did not answer.

"Have you forgotten our jade Buddha, then?"

"I have no time!" she repeated.

She put the tip of her handkerchief between her teeth and bit it. The old man stirred in his chair, but Siu-lan did not turn around.

I took a few steps away from her. I felt the old man's dead and bewitching eyes upon me, and I dared not look in his direction. With a physical certainty, I sensed his hatred poisoning the air I breathed.

"Then . . . then, Siu-lan, is it over?"

For a second I thought I wouldn't have the strength to finish this eternal and banal phrase.

The door opened and Li-Te appeared on the threshold.

"Dear friend," he said dryly, "I forgot to give you this invitation." He handed me a red card with large characters on it. "Don't fold it!" Li-Te said in a severe tone. "My father is inviting you to a formal banquet tonight."

"Is this the farewell banquet? I have to leave," I added, suddenly determined to get away.

Li-Te's mouth widened as if he were about to smile. "Yes," he said enigmatically. "A farewell banquet. It will be at his old friend Liang Ki's. You know . . . your friend from the boat."

I turned toward the old man; his eyes were alive again, gleaming in the shadow, yellow and phosphorescent as a tiger's.

I bowed deeply three times before him, in thanks. He made a polite nod and closed his eyes. Li-Te had vanished. Siu-lan had vanished. I went back to my room, afraid of my own solitude.

Burning tears welled in my eyes. "Alone! Alone!" I repeated, and forced myself to choke back my sobs.

"If I'm frightened," I suddenly realized, "I'm lost!" And I remembered my Eskimo guide the year before, in a northern country. Beside each other on the sled, we had climbed a deserted hill in the twilight. The earth was covered with snow, it was terribly cold and blue smoke came from the reindeer's nostrils.

At the summit we stopped for a moment. Before us, the tundra stretched as far as the eye could reach, hostile, terribly dead. My heart grew cold.

I turned toward my guide: "Aren't you frightened?" I asked him in Russian.

"If I'm frightened, I'm lost!" he answered calmly.

If I'm frightened, I'm lost! How many centuries had it taken these polar men to arrive at this heroic and practical method of overcoming fear! No recourse to the gods nor to the spirits of the ancestors. To control the imagination, to master fear, to pretend not to believe in it—that is the surest path. Ulysses knew this highest form of ruse.

I struggled to control my fluttering heart. I kept telling myself: "Siu-lan is going to leave . . . Siu-lan is going to leave. . . ."

And immediately a hideous solitude extended before me and I drove my rebellious heart onward.

Then I heard Siu-lan's footsteps approaching my door. The rustling of her silk gown, the click of her bracelets. The steps hesitated, came to a stop.

I could leap up, open the door, take Siu-lan's hand, force destiny to change its course. But I did not move, out of pride. Whatever happened, I would be ready.

The steps faded away very slowly, sliding across the matting. A door closed and everything returned to silence.

"I am ready!" I repeated to myself, and my body trembled from head to foot.

40

A MAN ROWED downstream on a great river.
For years on end, day and night he rowed, peering
at the horizon. Suddenly the current grew powerful, the man
lifted his head, cocked his ears: the river was a cataract,
there was no escape. Immediately he shipped his oars, crossed
his arms and began to sing.

I thought of that song and my heart beat faster. That is
the only hymn of freedom.

To vanquish hope, to realize that there is no escape, to
draw from this revelation an invincible joy—that is the
highest peak to which man may aspire.

I felt a tiger prowling around me and I was not frightened.
Suffering had petrified my heart, and every thought, even
the fiercest, seemed to me no more than a scarecrow.

The ricksha boy was drawing me as fast as he could run
toward the house of the old mandarin Liang Ki, where I
was invited for the banquet.

"All is lost!" I kept repeating to myself, with cruel insistence. "All is lost! Arise, my heart! This is the terrible moment to prove whether you are worthy of man!" A faint mist had enwrapped the huge city. I saw men, houses and trees through a transparent veil of tears.

"Siu-lan . . ." I murmured. "Siu-lan . . . Never again!"

I clenched my teeth and addressed myself with gentle severity: "Try to place your insignificant pain in the world's enormous pain; do not permit your individual case to assume absurd proportions! Be a man! Sing, now, the hymn of freedom!"

Joshiro's face appeared in the evening air. "How happy she must be!" I thought. "Happy, proud and free! With what an ascetic impulse she must have cast her body to that rabble of lustful generals, for a whole night! A city for a caress, a province for a cry of love. Devour my body. . . . Long live Japan!"

Her body in the service of a pitiless soul, Joshiro, eyes rolled back in her head, torn by the dogs of lust, the great, victorious martyr!

That young, bloodstained body on the threshold of a dreadful future filled me with remorse. ("Die well," Joshiro had shouted to me when we parted. I was wasting my life in unworthy and ephemeral joys! I was ashamed. My life had to change!)

Eyes closed, drawn through the Chinese streets by the coolie, I feverishly sketched the essential features of my time. I tried to find my post in order to fight and die at it:

1. The essential task of our times is the organization of two extreme camps.

2. A living man today is the one who takes an active part in this organization.

3. Right? Left? That has only a secondary importance. A question of temperament; reason, as is its custom, follows after and furnishes the arguments.

4. The two camps, whether they know it or not, collaborate. They are the thesis and antithesis which create, in their conflict, tomorrow's synthesis.

5. The more violent the conflict, the greater the chances of a rich synthesis. But also the more numerous the dangers. Nothing is sure.

6. To live this tragic uncertainty, to feel one's forces increase tenfold before it, that is the attitude most worthy of man in our period, the most fruitful human attitude.

7. To abandon larger divisions, for the moment. To concentrate all our efforts on a single point. To limit ourselves; obey; act! And play later!

"Play later . . . later . . ." I told myself, and I let my eyes linger on the streets of Peking. All this exotic beauty, the gold dragons, the colors, the temples, appeared like a lust dragging my soul to its perdition. . . .

Yes, delight in beauty is a mortal sin today. Kindness, sensitivity, patience are not the virtues of our time, but violence, impatience, the heroic and austere conception of life.

I love that war cry of the Scots highlanders: "Fight, resist, accept death!"

The ricksha stopped; a great carved door silently swung open. Kung Liang Ki was standing on the threshold, smiling.

"Deign to enter my humble house, O foreigner!" he said, bowing with exquisite ceremony.

We walked around Ing Pei and entered a huge garden filled with young shoots.

The Oriental coolness of that house, the inviolable gentleness and intimacy of private life, far from all strange eyes! Here women and waters and slender gazelles could leap up, far from the brutal street, happy.

"I am delighted to see you again," whispered the old lord in his honey-sweet, ironic voice. "And your little throng of tigers?" he added, laughing. "There were five, I think."

"All here," I answered gravely; "here, wounded and happy."

We went into the salon. Mandarins, old officers, Chinese diplomats—smiling, sly eyes, long, skillful hands. Kung Ta-hen, the old uncle, was there, smiling. But Li-Te . . . where was Li-Te?

On the walls, painted silk banners; in the corners, old bronze statuettes of robust and delicate workmanship. I caressed the greenish-bronze hair that swelled under my hand, the elegant storks, the mythological birds with crested heads.

The old mandarin proudly showed me all these marvels. He explained the title under a painting of inexpressible delicacy: "The evening bell chimes in a distant temple." Neither the temple nor the bell was shown: nothing but a calm, faintly gilded landscape, filled with a bluish haze.

A huge inscription on an old wooden plank hung in the place of honor, opposite the door.

"That is a famous manuscript," whispered my old host. "Notice the power of those lines, and yet their suppleness. A giant must have written those characters, a giant with a child's heart. And how marvelously the meaning is adapted to the form!"

Liang Ki, finger raised, slowly translated the mysterious characters for me:

"To be pure as the plum blossom, free as a bird, strong as an oak, supple as a willow; that is the Chinese ideal."

At this moment a giant mass of flesh appeared on the threshold: Siu-lan's father.

"Excuse me," my old friend murmured. "I must leave you a moment. It is in Kung T'ang Hen's honor that this dinner is being given; he is our guest this evening, even as the gods."

With his tiny steps he hurried toward the newcomer and humbly bowed three times before him. All the guests who were scattered in the garden or smoking on couches gathered together.

The old mandarin, standing on the threshold with a sad and distant smile, received their respects, murmuring something, doubtless a polite formula. For a moment he glanced about him as if he were looking for someone; he noticed me standing in a corner and fixed on me his black and weary eyes.

I hastened toward him and bowed slightly. He put out his hand, as if to keep me from paying him this respect. Out of politeness? Or contempt? Or hatred? I didn't know, but when I was about to touch his hand, he gently drew it away and crossed the threshold with his heavy and majestic stride.

He was given the place of honor, opposite the door; facing him, in the humblest place, sat the old lord giving the dinner. I sat at his right; Kung Ta-hen, the uncle, sat beside me; he smiled at me affectionately.

"What news?" I asked him in a murmur; "I've heard—"

"Everything's fine," he reassured me politely. "Fine."

The rarest delicacies were served, and the most precious drinks. Many times over we bowed before the silent old T'ang Hen and drank to his health; and he nodded slightly and smiled at us with mild grandeur.

The guests spoke in low tones, as if we were in a sickroom or a temple. Their faces were grave and smiling, a strange serenity spread over this ceremonial banquet.

For a moment or two the voices were raised in an animated discussion that spread from mouth to mouth. But almost at once everything returned to its earlier calm.

"What was that about?" I asked my old neighbor.

"We were discussing Sung art," he answered, his eyes still gleaming. "An art of greatness and exquisite sensitivity, noble, delicate, profoundly human. The center of every work of art in those days was man, human life, love, friendship, joy. Man was not annihilated, as in Buddhist art, by the contemplation of nirvana. He remained smiling and calm confronting the Universe, and he identified himself closely with its joys."

"What was the opinion of our guest Kung T'ang Hen?" I asked, curious to know the rhythm of his thought.

"He said nothing. He . . . he did not deign to take part in vain discussions. He is far away. . . ."

Around midnight the old mandarin who was giving the dinner stood up. He bowed three times before Siu-lan's father and drank in his honor, speaking a few words in a moved tone of voice.

Kung Ta-hen explained: "For long years, he looked at the sky and sighed for this evening. What an honor that so great a lord should deign to cross the threshold of his humble house! What a joy to open his eyes this evening and see him there!"

At the end of his speech, he added these old Chinese verses, fixing his eyes on Kung T'ang Hen:

> *Lo! the immortal, a lotus flower in his hand*
> *Departs for eternity by the invisible path!*

Siu-lan's old father stood up, his eyes fixed on the table. In a few words he praised the dishes, the house, the host, the guests.

Then he spoke of China; his voice trembled. Not everything he said was translated for me, but he spoke, I was told, of decadence, of protest, of slavery. He evoked the spirits of the ancestors, he opened his arms as if he wanted to embrace all China, the old, ravaged mother. . . .

Finally he recited in a quavering voice the famous verses of an old poet:

> *If Tao transformed my throat into a cockerel, I*
> *would announce the sunrise.*
> *If Tao turned my arm into a crossbow, I would*
> *aim at the foreigners and strike them down.*
> *If Tao made my body a chariot and my mind a*
> *horse, I would return, dear friends, to a*
> *happy and honored China!*

"So be it!"

Kung T'ang Hen sat down again, quite pale. The tea was

served. It was warm in the room and a window onto the garden was opened. The sweet smell of the earth penetrated the room.

Every face turned toward the trees of the garden, cottony in the moonlight. No one spoke.

"Life is beautiful," Kung T'ang Hen said, and stood up. The dinner was over.

We all rose; the servants opened the doors. We formed two rows to the right and left; the old Kung T'ang Hen passed slowly between us toward the door, and all bowed respectfully as he passed.

For a second he paused before me; he moved his lips as if he intended to say something. All listened intently, but he controlled himself, choked back the word or the cry, and continued his slow progress toward the great open door.

His mauve velvet litter was there and waiting for him; the old mandarin, upright on the threshold, was already putting out his foot when suddenly Kung Liang Ki broke away from our group, brandishing a long, curved saber. He leaped upon Siu-lan's father and with one blow cut off his head, with terrible strength.

The body staggered, blood spurted out high upon the door and the walls. A second, then the body rolled, noiselessly, like a heavy bundle of laundry, to the middle of the street.

The bearers bent down as if their master had stepped into the litter and ran off. Kung Liang Ki bowed to the ground and closed the door. The corpse remained in the dust.

I was shuddering with horror. "But why?" I shrieked, beside myself. "Why? Why have you killed him?"

The old mandarin, falling into the deep armchair that only a few moments before had been occupied by his dearly beloved friend, nodded and answered in a calm voice: "My venerable friend had resolved to seek death. Do not cry out, I beg you! He wanted to protest, by his death, against the occupation of his country by foreigners. He had begged me to help him in these last moments of his life. I loved him deeply and I agreed. Everything has been executed according to the strictest rites of our traditions."

And as I was still trembling at this bloody spectacle, the old mandarin smiled:

"White men," he said with a touch of scorn in his voice, "have an excessive fear of death. But why? If there is another life, my honorable friend is already there, happy; if not, at least this earth exists and the name of my venerable friend will never die again. In either case, he has played the little card of his life well. Wish me, I implore you, such a death as his!"

41

RETURNING TO the house at dawn, I saw Li-Te's window lit; I tiptoed across the garden and heard his voice and Siu-lan's, very distinct in the calm night.

I stopped for a moment, holding my breath. Did they know? Their voices sounded grave and calm. I went in silence to my own room, which was steeped in the lilac penumbra of the dawn. I opened the window; how calm the sky was, how inhuman and remote! And how ridiculous man makes himself, raising his arms to it!

"At least let us be worthy," I murmured. "Let us love, struggle and die standing!"

A strange pride suddenly welled up in me. The sensation of solitude tempered my heart like steel. I felt I was standing on a peak of force and despair, free.

To be alone, to turn solitude into a wellspring of strength and joy, to conquer, at last, both hope and fear—what happiness!

Finally, I had understood! I could scarcely contain a cry of triumph.

I made ready to go out into the street, reluctant to lose this inhuman joy of liberation in my sleep. But suddenly I heard footsteps in the hallway. Someone was approaching my door.

Was it Siu-lan? My heart began to pound. The resolute steps came nearer. I quickly walked to the door; someone had scratched on it. I opened it and Li-Te stood before me.

"Li-Te!" I exclaimed, ready to throw myself into his arms. "Li-Te, do you know?"

"Don't raise your voice," Li-Te said, lifting one hand. "I know."

A few seconds of silence. Li-Te walked into the room and closed the door behind him. He stood before me, crossed his arms and looked into my eyes. The tender morning light clung to his wrinkled brow, his pale cheeks; but his eyes were still in darkness.

"Li-Te," I murmured, unable to endure the silence a moment longer, "will you tell me something?"

Li-Te clenched his teeth; his lips parted and he muttered a word I did not hear.

"What did you say?"

"Get out!"

I threw back my head. Rage and sadness choked me. The words couldn't leave my throat. I felt my nails digging deep into the palms of my hands.

Li-Te recovered his composure first. "Forgive me," he said in a calm and firm voice. "But it is necessary."

"I'll leave at once!" I said at last.

The fury had vanished; only the sadness still gripped my throat.

Li-Te thought a moment, his eyes on the inscription over the door. "No," he said, "wait until tomorrow. You must say goodbye to my sister anyway. She'll be leaving too."

"You have no pity for her?" I exclaimed, without thinking.

I was ashamed at once, but it was too late. Li-Te frowned but made no reply. "Sleep well," he said slowly. "And forgive me."

He was already leaving, crossing the threshold. I no longer held myself back. "Li-Te!" I exclaimed. "Li-Te, dear friend of my youth, then . . . then it's all over?"

"Yes," he answered gravely.

"Without a word of regret or affection? Nothing? Nothing?"

"I have no time," Li-Te answered, exactly like his sister. "I have no time. I have other tigers to tame. Forgive me."

He bowed politely and left, closing the door gently.

"I have other tigers too!" I cried, alone. "I don't need your affection. I don't need anyone. I'm free!"

I felt an inhuman cruelty toward myself, a hideous joy in agony and in mastering agony.

Like the samurai who, mortally wounded on the battle-field, composed heroic verses to greet death with, I suddenly longed to cast into this night of anguish a savage chant of freedom.

I, the human heart, am the militant God who battles on the frontiers. I, the human heart, am the commander-in-chief of all powers, visible and invisible.

I believe in the heart of man, that earthen threshing-floor where, night and day, life battles with death.

"Help me!" you shout, O my heart, and I hear.

Blessed be all those who hear and rush to free you, O heart of man, and who say: "Only you and I exist."

Blessed be all those who have freed you, O heart of man, and who say: "You and I are one."

And thrice blessed be those who do not buckle under, but bear this great, this terrifying secret: "Even this One does not exist."

I felt delivered. A free man. I closed my eyes and slept for a few hours, a calm, light sleep; no dream dared approach my bed and trouble my happiness.

Around ten I leaped out of bed. On my desk was an empty box of Japanese cigarettes; inside the box I read these words written in an eager but firm hand: *Do not try to save me. I want to die. I have performed my duty to the end. I am happy, O white friend. I wish you such a death as mine!*

I left these proud lines on my desk and went out into the garden. Siu-lan and Li-Te were already there, standing together, murmuring to each other, their faces grave and serene. I could discern a gently exalted expression, a strange radiance. Evidently they were both far from any personal concern; I was sure they were speaking of their country and making decisions.

Siu-lan was wearing a cloak; a little suitcase was at her feet. Li-Te must have been giving her final instructions. And Siu-lan, her head raised, listened with a concentration that altered and hardened her features.

How free she was from any selfish or petty preoccupation! Her individual suffering had assumed its true proportions, lost like a tiny sigh over the immense and dolorous face of China!

I felt the spirit of the old, dead father prowling in his garden, caressing these two beloved faces. He must have been happy, that spirit liberated at last from his burdensome body; he saw his children following the path traced by his desire; he felt that Siu-lan was saved, and that the white man was vanquished.

I walked toward them steadily. Li-Te watched me approach, impassive; his face was polite and firm. Siu-lan, with a slow gesture, smoothed a lock of hair on her forehead. She lay her hand on her throat and lowered her head a little.

With almost painful clarity I heard the buzzing of a bee as it pushed into a wisteria cluster over her head. At the corner of the garden, in front of the gate, I saw the old father's armchair still there, empty, disturbing; I could make out, down to the smallest details, the interlaced dragons carved on the back.

Finally Li-Te raised his voice: "Dear friend, Siu-lan is leaving."

He stopped—just long enough for me to hear a rustling sound in my heart, a sound like that of silk tearing.

"She didn't want to leave, though," he continued, "without saying goodbye to you."

Then Siu-lan took a step and, with her hands crossed on her breast, bowed before me.

I bowed too, just as deeply, three times. I wanted to cry out: "Siu-lan!" But the name did not come out; I felt myself choking on it. I wanted to smile, but my lips would not obey me; my face remained tense and hard.

Siu-lan picked up the little suitcase; a ricksha boy, the man with the scar, stopped in front of the old red-painted door.

Li-Te shook his sister's hand. "I cannot come with you," he said, and again said nothing. Then suddenly he murmured, "Come back soon, Siu-lan," almost moved.

Siu-lan bowed again, very slender and pale, supple as a branch of weeping willow, and disappeared.

$\mathcal{N}$oon. A rock garden in an old cloister. Not one flower, not one green leaf, not one drop of water. Trees and flowers blossom outside the high, austere wall, within reach of the crowd.

This garden is a desert of sand, and on this sand some fifteen rocks, large and small, are scattered as though by chance. The Chinese poet who arranged it this way three centuries ago had a specific intention: to suggest the image of a fleeing tiger.

And indeed, one suddenly feels these rocks are panic-stricken, thrust aside and overturned as if a terrible and invisible being were leaping from one to the other and shaking them to their roots.

A tiger, or death, or love, or God.

I wander through this garden under the perpendicular light, and vague desires are gradually illuminated within me, crystallizing around a hard core.

I no longer care about the Beginning or the End of things.

I no longer make any suppositions. I scorn all hope, and all comfortable cowardice.

I dig in the earth, this field of ours. I see with my eyes, I touch with my hands: from the inorganic mass to the plant, from the plant to the animal, from the animal to man.

Someone or something, over millions of centuries, mounts, mounts, painfully mounts.

I would follow its rhythm, mount with it, outstrip my parents, myself, at every moment blazing a trail in my heart and head for that someone or something that mounts. . . .

To be rid of poetry, sensibility, tenderness, happiness!

To face—without any mirage of beauty, kindness or fear—our dreadful and sublime reality.

To compose a free heart, in the image of this rock garden!

N.K., Aegina, 1936

'Vivid, potent, beautifully measured, and sustained by astonishingly deft description . . . a wonderful book'

Independent on Sunday

'In *This Side of Brightness*, there is more than superb writing. There is strong visualisation of character . . . A novel that truly represents and reveres the incredible strength of the powerless' *Irish Tatler*

'With extraordinary economy McCann constructs a narrative of sadness and small victories, of laughter and devastating tragedy . . . He is that rare creature, a real writer'

Irish Independent

'The language you find in Colum McCann's novel, *This Side of Brightness*, makes you claw yourself with pleasure . . . It is, perhaps, the first authentic novel about homelessness, about living below and beyond this rich city. And you know Colum McCann has been there, he evokes so powerfully the stink of the present, the poignancy of the past'

Frank McCourt author of *Angela's Ashes*

'Highly original, moving and impressive' *Time Out*

'*This Side of Brightness* is McCann's finest achievement to date, a *tour de force* . . . It's a confident, intricate work which gradually draws seemingly diffuse strands together . . . It's a quality of McCann's confidence and skill that he judges his own pace, withholding information almost to the last to create his extraordinary jigsaw . . . this novel establishes McCann firmly as one of the finest writers of his generation . . . *This Side of Brightness* is a richly memorable and deeply impressive achievement'

Dermot Bolger, *Sunday Independent*

Colum McCann was born in Dublin in 1965. He has lived in America, Japan and Ireland, and divides his time between Dublin and New York City. He was awarded the 1994 Rooney Prize for Irish Literature for his short story collection *Fishing the Sloe-Black River*, and he is currently adapting his first novel, *Songdogs*, for the screen.

BY THE SAME AUTHOR

Fishing the Sloe-Black River
Songdogs